SIX SERMONS

ON THE

INSPIRATION OF HOLY SCRIPTURE.

THE LETTER AND THE SPIRIT.

Six Sermons

ON THE

INSPIRATION OF HOLY SCRIPTURE,

PREACHED BEFORE THE UNIVERSITY OF OXFORD IN THE DISCHARGE
OF HIS OFFICE OF SELECT PREACHER.

BY

CHARLES P. CHRETIEN, M.A.
RECTOR OF CHOLDERTON, FELLOW AND LATE TUTOR OF ORIEL.

"Let us follow after the things which make for peace, and things wherewith one may edify another."

WIPF & STOCK · Eugene, Oregon

Wipf and Stock Publishers
199 W 8th Ave, Suite 3
Eugene, OR 97401

The Letter and the Spirit
Six Sermons on the Inspiration of Holy Scripture,
Preached Before the University of Oxford
in the Discharge of His Office of Select Preacher
By Chretien, Charles P.
Softcover ISBN-13: 978-1-6667-6067-5
Hardcover ISBN-13: 978-1-6667-6068-2
eBook ISBN-13: 978-1-6667-6069-9
Publication date 10/3/2022
Previously published by Macmillan and Co., 1961

This edition is a scanned facsimile of
the original edition published in 1961.

TO

EDWARD HAWKINS, D.D.

PROVOST OF ORIEL,

AND IRELAND PROFESSOR OF EXEGESIS,

THIS VOLUME IS INSCRIBED,

NOT IN THE CONFIDENCE THAT HE WILL WHOLLY

APPROVE OF ITS CONTENTS,

BUT IN THE HOPE

THAT HE WILL ACCEPT ITS DEDICATION TO HIM

AS A TOKEN

OF THE WRITER'S GRATEFUL ESTEEM AND REGARD.

C. S.

PREFACE.

WHATEVER faults the reader may find in the substance of the following pages, they do not arise from haste on the part of the writer. He committed to writing the principal thoughts contained in them nearly nine years ago. But on reflection he was not sure that an occasion had arrived on which those thoughts would be useful. He therefore suppressed them for the time, though believing them to be substantially true.

The last few years, however, have greatly altered the general state of feeling and information with regard to Holy Scripture. There is now no longer the same unthinking assent, even on the part of many thinking minds, to sweeping and unproved assertions as to its nature and functions. Enquiry on these subjects has now become a necessity; and our choice lies only between an enquiry conducted in a calm and reverent spirit, and a rash and hasty enquiry, which does not trust itself to the Truth, but begins by assuming its conclusions, and spends the rest of its time in looking about for arguments to support them. The writer, at the suggestion of several friends, availing himself of the opportunity afforded him by his appointment as select preacher, has attempted, in the following Sermons, to shew that the necessary researches may be conducted without the distraction of painful doubts and the bitterness of excited controversy. It will be to him a source of real gratitude should he find that he has at all succeeded in this aim. He has certainly had the wish, even should it prove that he has not the power, to comfort anxious souls who are struggling for life among deep waters. It is a task in which those have not succeeded, who float on their own light theories above the mysterious depths, and fancy that their line has fathomed them.

Apart from errors in the matter of these Sermons, from which the writer is well aware that he cannot expect to be exempt, he is conscious of many defects in their form. These arise less from want of pains than of skill. He found it exceedingly difficult in a series of discourses, delivered to a varying audience at uncertain intervals during two years, to keep each clear, without allowing any to be one-sided. The latter fault he was particularly anxious to avoid. If he has succeeded, it may be at the price of some repetition and obscurity. But he hopes that a fairly careful perusal of the volume will not leave much uncertainty as to its meaning.

The few Notes which are appended to the Sermons contain some quotations, and vindicate some lines of thought, which the writer was unwilling to leave without notice, though he could not conveniently incorporate them with the text.

It is the Author's earnest prayer, that if this volume cannot forward the Truth of God, it may have no power to hinder it. May God give to His Church, in this and other difficult matters, not the spirit of fear, or of anger, which is often a disguised form of fear, but of power, and love, and of a sound mind.

CONTENTS.

SERMON I.

Preached at St Mary's Church, 20 Nov. 1859.

HOLY SCRIPTURE THE INSTRUMENT OF THE HOLY SPIRIT.

PAGE

2 TIM. III. 16, 17.—All Scripture is given by inspiration of God, and is profitable for doctrine, for reproof, for correction, for instruction in righteousness: that the man of God may be perfect, throughly furnished unto all good works 1

SERMON II.

Preached at St Mary's Church, 18 March, 1860.

THE UNITY OF HOLY SCRIPTURE TO BE LOOKED FOR IN ITS SPIRIT AND PURPOSE.

JOHN VII. 17.—If any man will do his will, he shall know of the doctrine, whether it be of God, or whether I speak of myself 27

SERMON III.

THE DIFFICULTY OF APPROACHING THE INSPIRATION OF HOLY SCRIPTURE THROUGH THE INSPIRATION OF ITS WRITERS.

Preached at St Mary's Church, 20 May, 1860.

2 PETER I. 21.—For the prophecy came not in old time by the will of man: but holy men of God spake as they were moved by the Holy Ghost 58

SERMON IV.

Preached in Christ Church Cathedral, 21 Oct. 1860.

THE SHADOW OF THE LAW DETERMINED BY THE SUBSTANCE OF THE GOSPEL.

PAGE

COLOSSIANS II. 17.—Which are a shadow of things to come; but the body is of Christ 8

SERMON V.

Preached at Christ Church Cathedral, 16 Dec. 1860.

CHRIST, THE CENTRE OF CHRISTIAN TRUTH.

I JOHN III. 24.—Hereby we know that he abideth in us, by the Spirit which he hath given us 116

SERMON VI.

Preached at St Mary's Church, 9 June, 1861.

THE METHOD OF LOVE.

I CORINTHIANS VIII. 1—3.—Knowledge puffeth up, but charity edifieth. And if any man think that he knoweth any thing, he knoweth nothing yet as he ought to know. But if any man love God, the same is known of him . . 140

NOTES 163

SERMON I.

HOLY SCRIPTURE, THE INSTRUMENT OF THE HOLY SPIRIT.

Preached at St Mary's Church, 20 Nov. 1859.

2 TIM. III. 16, 17.

All scripture is given by inspiration of God, and is profitable for doctrine, for reproof, for correction, for instruction in righteousness: that the man of God may be perfect, throughly furnished unto all good works.

IF we acknowledge, as acknowledge we must, that great causes are meant to lead to great effects, and that things have a purpose, there is one nation, the purpose of whose existence and history we can have little difficulty in determining. Few facts are more clear and patent than the special mission of the Jews. Of all the branches of the great human family, they are marked with an impression the most unmistakeably Divine. To them was entrusted, in spite of all their sins and rebellions, the privilege of teaching to the world the Truth of God. Traitors and idolators as they often were, they still could not help proclaiming—proclaiming by their sufferings and punishments when their tongues were silent—that there was one God, who had created man, and had entered into relations with man His creature. Their work did not end, till, after a long preparation of the hearts and minds of men for that great event, the relation between God and man became most close and intimate, when the Son of God revealed Himself as the Son of man, and the Word became Flesh, and dwelt among us. The Jewish tradition then ceased, not by becoming untrue, but by becoming universal. The arms of Rome and the arts of Greece had prepared the soil to receive the seed which had been committed to the chosen people. The Spirit of God, working by ways which we know not, or know imperfectly at the best, took from the casket the treasure which had hitherto been hidden in it, and made the unwilling Jew the preacher of good tidings to the willing Gentile. The sacred race had been entrusted with a dispensation which they obeyed through their rebellion, and fulfilled in the act of renouncing it. God then poured that Spirit upon all flesh which had hitherto been working most powerfully upon a particular nation. The wisdom and power of this world were humbled at the foot of the Cross. By the light of that Cross, in which he had learned to glory, St Paul was allowed in his measure to see whence the Spirit was coming and whither it was going. Unseen itself, he could trace its course in its effects; by its working on his own inspired mind, by the bend and turn of events, and the bowing of the hearts of nations. It was going from the Jews to the Gentiles; from a part to the whole, from a nation to the world. Blessed with this new and precious knowledge, St Paul still held in his hands and retained in his mind that sacred volume, so dear to his youth, and of which he had found the key in his manhood; so closely associated with the history of his race, and the dealings of God towards it; full of record, and prophecy, and moral teaching, and Divine song, all meeting with their completion, and tending to their end, in Christ. No wonder that he taught that this Scripture was profitable for doctrine, for reproof, for correction, for instruction in righteousness; no wonder that he pronounced it *inspired*[1].

It could scarcely have entered into the mind of St Paul, when he wrote those important words to Timothy, announcing the inspiration of the Old Testament, that they would hereafter be accepted by the Church as themselves possessing a like inspiration, and forming a part of the Scriptures of the new covenant. He knew indeed his high mission as an apostle, and what Spirit it was that guided his words. In his very earliest epistle he wrote thus to the Thessalonians: "for this cause also thank we God without ceasing, because, when ye received the word of God which ye heard of us, ye

[1] Note I.

received it not as the word of men, but as it is in truth, the word of God, which effectually worketh also in you that believe[1]." There is no reason to doubt that he recognised in his own written teaching, the same Divine element which he recognised in his unwritten words. Still there is no proof that he was aware of the part which he was taking in forming the New Testament Canon, when he wrote a letter to a church or an individual. It would be rash to say that he knew how much the inspiration of the Old Testament would in after time be rested on the authority of his own inspired declaration concerning it. We know that his thoughts were fixed on spreading the Gospel of Christ; we do not know that they were consciously devoted to forming a body of written documents which should record and contain it. Nothing however can be more natural than that his writings should be an integral portion of the later and more precious written covenant. As the Jewish Scriptures reveal a part of the counsel of God, so he

[1] 1 Thess. ii. 13.

declared the whole[1]; as the Old Testament writings contain a peculiar dispensation, his epistles disclose an universal one. Those documents are inspired, which tell of the time when the choicest blessings of God were confined within narrow bounds; those documents are also inspired, which show us the waters of grace overflowing their old channels, and streaming from the Jew to the Gentile.

It is with a deep sense of the importance and difficulty of the subject, that I venture to lay before you on the present occasion some remarks on the structure and inspiration of Holy Scripture, to be continued, if it please God, in following sermons. Theories, even those which are plausible or probable, I shall endeavour as much as possible to avoid. I would rather try to place before you, in what appears to me a real and obvious connection, some of the main facts concerning Holy Scripture, and our position with regard to it. Our enquiries will naturally be made in more immediate connection with the New Testament.

[1] Acts xx. 27.

Our knowledge of the authors who wrote it, and of the circumstances under which it was written, though very far from complete, is much fuller than any similar knowledge which we have with regard to the Old Testament. If we examine its structure in connection with the system of which it forms a part, and with our relation to that system, we may make no new or startling discoveries, and yet be led to conclusions of considerable practical value.

The Gospel was in existence before the New Testament began. We can mark one most important point in connection with St Paul's life, which is antecedent to the very germ of the Canon. No Gospel or Epistle was written at the time of his conversion[1]. There are few more indisputable events in the history of the world than that on a certain day, Saul, afterwards Paul, while journeying on the errand of persecution from Jerusalem to Damascus, was struck to the ground, and rose an altered man. Those who can read his life, and his letters to the churches,

[1] Note II.

and trace the part which his doctrine has since played in the history of the world, without seeing a Divine Hand in his conversion, must refuse to see it anywhere. He soon became an able minister of the New Testament, not of the letter, but of the Spirit. In the written letter, that Testament did not then exist. We may not be able to determine with a certainty the exact order in which its component books were written; but we know that the First Epistle to the Thessalonians is certainly among the earliest. It contains, at its close, a very valuable indication of the manner in which the New Testament Canon was formed: "I charge you by the Lord," thus wrote St Paul at the close of the epistle, "that this Epistle be read unto all the holy brethren[1]." The detached portions of the New Testament gradually gathered round the infant Church. Book after book, with or without definite authority, was read in the congregation. By no technical law, it would seem, but in obedience to a deep and hidden instinct, the

[1] 1 Thess. v. 27.

writings of apostles and holy men were brought together, and joined into a volume.

The time came ere long when a new process was to begin. The Church began to examine more closely the contents of the sacred volume which she had collected. So far as we can judge, the New Scriptures were no longer the exponents of a Divine Life burning brightly and freshly in the Church. *They* spoke the same language, and breathed the same thoughts as ever; but men heard them not with the same feelings: the first spirit of the Apostolic times was gone. The second stage had arrived, when men, from simply feeling with those early writings, and sending their hearts spontaneously with them, looked at them, in some measure, from without, were anxious to see what they contained and proved, and therefore, of necessity, criticised them. It became a question of importance, what books should, and what should not, be admitted into the Canon. The Churches left no means at their disposal unemployed for ascertaining the truth in this matter. They pondered long and enquired widely. They used both external and internal evidence; but they seem to have placed their chief reliance on definite historical testimony. About several books they long doubted, and, even when they received them at last, left some points doubtful about them. Thus was the Canon constructed in different parts of Christendom, with a wonderful agreement in all its general features, though with differences, to the last, about some particular books[1]. And then—the old ties gave way: the East was at discord with the West: the Church was torn asunder, and the corporate action of its disunited parts became impossible. In all this disunion, however, the parts still looked back to the time when they were united in a living whole; and, in all disputes about Apostolic doctrine and practice, turned for information to those inspired books, which both by their contents and their associations recalled the happy period, when the faith and hope and communion of the Church were *One*.

The New Testament, then, when consi-

[1] Note III.

dered in connection with its history, must be regarded as the most enduring form, but not as the only form, of Christian doctrine. The first teachers taught by word of mouth, as well as by writing. The first hearers were, as we have seen, praised, not blamed, by an Apostle, because they received his *spoken* word as the word of God. When the first impulse of Christian teaching began to fail, and the body of the Church was divided, the written word occupied the place of direct Apostolic teaching, because it alone could be had. A Roman or a Corinthian Christian, for instance, if in later days he wished to ascertain, on any point, the truth of Christ, could not adopt a wiser course than to turn to the New Testament volume, and read in its pages how St Paul had, on the point in question, as the follower of Christ, taught his Christian forefathers. And we in these last days, when we seek to renew in our hearts the image of Christ, and in our minds the doctrines of His gospel, turn with a sure instinct to the precious records which those earliest times have left us—to the simple teaching of the uneducated Galilæan, to the fervid eloquence of the Apostle of the Gentiles, to the sublime devotion of St John. Yet these writings we take not primarily as the writings of St Matthew, or St Paul, or St John, but as the inspired Word of God. We call them inspired, because His Spirit breathes through them now. We know that He breathes through them, not only by present experience and observation, but by their connection with the history of the past. For the Bible does not stand alone. We do not find it lying, in awful and mysterious isolation, like an antique pillar, covered with strange hieroglyphics, on the shores of time. It stands in the closest and most obvious relation to the present state of the world, and its past religious experience. It is the word of God, for it tells us of the work of God, and does the work of God even now. It is the enduring form in which God has been pleased to cast the Gospel which existed before it. It is, together with Christendom, the great document of Christianity. The Church is the work of God; the Bible is the word of

God. In it, He, through human instruments, has written, in His way, His will. In it, we, reading what He has written, decipher His will towards us. The human instrument was necessary to write, just as the human eye and mind are necessary to read; but it is the Word of God, and not of man.

It may be worth while considering, whether this is not the best way to approach the subject of Inspiration—to consider the Bible as itself the Inspired Word through which God speaks to our spirits. As an inspired Word, it was written by inspired men; but the first truth *to us* is *its* inspiration, not *theirs*. There is another method of approaching this subject, in which this order is inverted. The Bible is not viewed primarily as an inspired whole, in reference to the declared purposes and counsels of God; but it is divided into parts, and their inspiration is referred severally to the minds of their separate authors. It is of course no valid objection to this view of the subject, that it involves difficulties. We must expect to find difficulties in the Bible. Revelation only relieves us from one class of difficulties, on condition that we accept another. It throws a light from heaven about our daily path, but leaves us seeing things at a distance through a glass darkly. If the Bible contained and implied no difficulties at all, it would be singularly unlike the other works of God. The great objection to the view in question lies in the *nature* of the difficulties which it raises. It engages the enquirer in an investigation which is impossible for many and difficult for all. As a step to accepting the Bible as a whole, it would lead us to enquire who wrote each particular book, and what evidence we have of the author's inspiration. It would be hard, possibly it is not desirable, to explain to those who have not made trial of such investigations, how many perplexities beset them. They place the enquirer in an unnatural position, outside the truth which he loves. A mind of ordinary power and learning stands simply aghast before them. They require a linguistic and technical apparatus which few could acquire with the labour of a life, and fewer still could employ when gained. These questions will of course exist, whatever view we take of Inspiration. But it is better, surely, if it is possible, to throw them into their proper place, at the circumference, not at the centre, of Christian truth, where they may exist as proofs of our ignorance and trials of our humility, but cannot occur as obstacles to our faith. Surely the student of divinity, as well as the child and the peasant, has a right, antecedent to all such enquiries, and independent of them, to take up the Bible as the Word of God, and read it for his instruction and comfort.

It is the nature of a book, or of a written word, that through it one mind exercises an influence on another. Through it, impressions are conveyed from intelligence to intelligence, which, if not exactly alike, bear at least some real relation and analogy to each other. Could we imagine an inscription or a poem to be produced by a chance collocation of letters, independently of any presiding mind, we could not call it the written word of any intelligence whatsoever. Through it, mind would not speak to mind; the reader would give it all its meaning. But it is not in this relation that we find ourselves standing to any part of the universe. Everywhere about us are the traces of an Intelligence, independent of and above our own. Everywhere, humility is a learner poring over a lesson, and science a gatherer of pebbles on the shore of the ocean of truth. Not least, but rather most is this the case, when man, turning from the interests and facts of the material universe, looks at his own consciousness, and enquires respecting his great and wonderful destiny—what is his origin, and his tendency, and his work, and his hope. To questions such as these, philosophy returns a guess for answer, and nature sends back an ambiguous reply, in which her voice is blended with the echo of our own hopes and fears. But faith receives a far more clear, though still a partial answer, as she accepts the revelation which was made by the Incarnate Son of God, and is recorded in His inspired Word.

But how do we know the Bible to be the

Word of God? Both by testimony, and by the answer of its Spirit to our spirit—by external authority, and by its own. These may not weigh equally with different classes of minds. The gift of 'discerning of spirits' is not given in like measure to all. Nor does it follow that those who make the greatest claims to spiritual discernment possess the faculty most fully. Yet the argument from its wonderful adaptation to human nature is not lightly to be thrown aside. Few indeed would adopt in this day the extreme hypothesis, so common two centuries ago, according to which the believer possessed a spiritual sense, which enabled him to determine what was Holy Scripture and what was not, without any appeal to external authority. Such authority was then, for reasons of which we are well aware, looked upon with undue suspicion. To trust to a human authority, whether corporate or individual, merely *as* human, is indeed foreign to the spirit of the Gospel. In this way, we may call no man master. But human authority gains a very powerful sanction, when regarded as a form of the

Divine providence. 'The Powers that be are ordained of God.' To submit to such authority may be merely an endeavour to avoid thought and escape responsibility; but it may also be a sign of reliance on God's providence, an act of faith and conscientious obedience. If it be argued, as it often is, that this reliance on the external guidance of God would lead heathens to remain heathens, and perpetuate the breaches of Christendom, by letting error enclose itself in its own shell, and harden itself for ever—it may be replied, that it seems the will of God to limit the power of man to attain truth, not only by the temper of mind in which he seeks it, but by the conditions under which he makes the search. The history of the Jewish dispensation—that long, gradual, halting, irregular advance towards the truth of Christ—may teach us how much our true wisdom lies in waiting, and how consistent real holiness is with imperfect knowledge. Even those who sit in darkness and the shadow of death may, if they look warily and walk innocently, see some beams of the true light playing on the edge of the shadow. Those who have studied the language which St Paul used when speaking either to Jews or Gentiles of the condition of the heathen, will entertain the hope that the good among them had, through the working of God's Spirit, some sense of their brotherhood in Him, though knowing nothing of Christ the head; and that the work of the law was not written on their hearts in vain. Surely there is nothing unholy or unscriptural in the feeling which makes us begin by believing that our country, our Church, our family, our teachers are given us by God, and have the first claim upon us. Almost all the converts who have been a blessing to the world are those on whom the truth has beamed after long and patient waiting for it, not men who have detached themselves from their communion, because it was no home for them. Those who have done so, whatever have been their other gifts and graces, have generally gone on to change after change—changing at last no longer only because they have been driven in their progress to some ultimate point of opinion, at which, without self-contradiction, further change became impossible[1].

Hitherto we have spoken of the Word of God, as it appears to man when he regards it by its own light, and the light of God's present providence. But man, especially educated man, is obliged by the law of his nature to look both backward and forward. Forward, his unassisted powers can look a very little way indeed; backward, he is led in the study of history. He seeks the causes of the present in the past. With a deep and living interest, he looks back through the centuries to the foundation of his dearest hopes. As he studies the history of the Christian Church, be passes through the long vista of years, often dark with ignorance and stained with blood, yet also often showing, both in communities and individuals, the brightness and the glory of the Lord. At length he comes nearer to that centre of light, from which all the scattered glories which he has seen, radiate. There, in a group, not seen all with equal distinctness, stand round one centre

[1] Note IV.

Apostle, Evangelist, and Saint. More clearly marked than the rest, stand out the features of the divine St John, and the zealous visage of St Paul. But the eye does not stay here. By Paul and John it passes on to Christ. There, at His Cross, we find, in all the obscurity produced by its own transcendent brightness, the mystery of godliness manifested in the flesh. We see His great works, we contemplate His life and death: we look at the empty sepulchre; by faith we behold the risen form. Thank God that it is not a privilege denied us, that rather it is our express and bounden duty, to fall down and worship.

I have endeavoured, however imperfectly, to lay before you some remarks on a way in which we may, without any presumption, approach that important subject—the Inspiration of Holy Scripture. We have regarded it as the permanent form into which God has been pleased to throw the record, first of His dealings with His chosen people, next, of the life on earth of his only-begotten Son, and lastly, of His Providence toward the early

Church, at a time when the light was burning brightly within it, before the sins and infirmities of men had impaired its unity, and scattered into a multitude of broken lights the glories of the body of Christ. And be this remembered, when we read the Bible, that we have in the written Word a book which is not only of the past, but of the present. In a common book of any antiquity, we trace the mind of one who is no longer with us. The thoughts that we read, flashed through the brain of a man like ourselves, it may be hundreds of years ago. He is gone: his old thoughts are, in his changed state of being, probably not his present thoughts: we converse through his writings with a mind which *was*, rather than with a mind which *is*. Not so, when we read the Word of God. The living Spirit then stirs beneath the letter which else were dead: the Infinite mind reveals itself, according to its will and our capacity, to our minds.

Thoughts like these can scarcely be unfitting, when, in the spirit of devotion and prayer, we approach the study of Holy Scripture. They are meant to embody no theory concerning it; but rather to remind us, with Holy Scripture itself, that it is inspired; with the Church of England, that it contains all things necessary to salvation. They do not put in the foreground those difficulties which are felt with regard to the structure and condition of its human framework; but place them in a position where, if we are called on to approach them at all, we can approach them without unsettling the first principles of our faith. They call us away from difficult and perhaps unprofitable questions as to the letter, to a closer search after the Spirit. Those only who find that Spirit, which was before the letter, in the letter, read the Bible aright. How much it is meant to teach them on some subjects, they may not know: but this they know, that if they are blest to discover it, all saving truth is there. They will come to the Scriptures to learn, through the Spirit, of Christ. As through the Sacraments, in a way we know not of, and do not presume to define, the wells of grace are opened, and the waters flow forth to the Christian congregation; so, through the Word, in the fulness of spiritual efficacy, the waters of grace distil to the individual soul. In either case there is a human instrument with a Divine commission; but in either case also the loving and reverent heart ascends through the instrument to God. And as our faith and love should rest on Christ, it may be that our knowledge also is safest when turned to Him. The researches of history, the apparatus of criticism, the theories which we bring to bear upon the whole or part of His Word, may be innocent and useful in their place. But their proper place seems to be after, not before, the Divine knowledge. That knowledge, we doubt not, is possible to the unlearned and ignorant as well as to the wise; that knowledge, in the wise, must rest on the same foundations as it does in the unlearned and ignorant. Its root is faith, a faith which clings humbly and hopefully to the foot of the Cross, and, having found its home there, cares not to wander from it. It is because the Old Testament tells of this as well as the New, that it is profitable for doctrine, for reproof, for correction, for instruction in righteousness. It is because the Scriptures have been framed by the Spirit for these holy purposes, and serve through His operations to that holy purpose still, that we pronounce them, with the Apostle, inspired.

Holy Scripture has been compared of old to a musical instrument. If we follow out the hint supplied by the Greek word, we may perhaps compare it to an organ. One in its purpose, it is yet most complex in its structure. Its different portions, fashioned by divers hands, working for the most part independently, combine to a common purpose, because the operation of each and all is directed by one presiding mind. All the parts may not appear in themselves equally essential or elaborate: yet we dare not declare any of them imperfect, because they have been placed where they are by Him who has designed the whole. Some notes seem by comparison thin and feeble; but they have doubtless their place in the Divine harmony. Much of the vocal machine is often silent: as we listen, a single note streams forth in the simplicity of clearness; or a gentle breath of sound is heard in front of a deep and muttering harmony; or a whole flood of music bursts forth in triumphant joy. We hearken in wonder and in awe; for no common will moves in the mighty Instrument. He who fashioned the world and our souls, has made it by the hand of His creatures; He, the Lord of spirits, has poured His Spirit within it. Through it He speaks, in the condescension of Infinite Power, to our spirits. He has placed it where it stands, to fill with its mighty music a temple older than itself, the Church of the living God.

SERMON II.

THE UNITY OF HOLY SCRIPTURE TO BE LOOKED FOR IN ITS SPIRIT AND PURPOSE.

Preached at St Mary's Church, 18 March, 1860.

JOHN VII. 17.

If any man will do his will, he shall know of the doctrine, whether it be of God, or whether I speak of myself.

IN a former Sermon from this place, I endeavoured to describe a manner, in which the soul of the Christian, guided by the providence of God, might, without any disturbance of the attitude of Faith and Trust, be taught to connect the present with the past, and explore its own intellectual position, without departing from the Cross of Christ. The inspiration of Holy Scripture was referred to in this connection. Holy Scripture was viewed as the instrument through which the Holy Spirit works on the heart of man now, and records His work in former ages. The evidence of its inspiration was sought, not in any examination of the state of mind in which individual men wrote the several books, but in the connection of the Bible with the entire structure and organism of Christianity. The nature of this inspiration would, on the same principles, be a matter not of previous assumption, but for after enquiry. "This book, as well as the Gospel which it records and perpetuates, is from God:"—such is the verdict of the ordinary human judgment. "The Divine element in this book is traceable in these particulars, may be ascribed to these secondary causes, necessitates this or that peculiarity in its composition:"—such questions as these latter with regard to the Bible, ordinary people, happily, can do without, though a strong necessity may urge a few to investigate them. The important truths contained in the former and simpler positions are not dependent upon any theories involved in the latter. These theories, however, in their place, it would be idle to condemn as useless, impossible to exclude as mischievous. Neither indifference nor rash assumption is the right posture of mind with regard to questions, confessedly difficult and perplexing, and yet connecting themselves closely with the dearest and most mysterious interests of humanity. Questions they are which in these days the patent facts of the world prompt many to ask, while none perhaps have sufficient data for answering them. But we may feel after a truth which we cannot fully grasp; and there are few, if any, subjects, on which it it is not better that men should enquire reverently and humbly, even at the risk of error, than that they should agree, for fear of possible consequences, to leave them altogether uninvestigated. If, indeed, like many apparently abstract questions, they have, at root, a practical bearing, it is vain to profess to exclude them from the field of enquiry. Our very reserve about them involves an assumption of their nature; and our acts prejudge them when our lips are silent. To forbid enquiry respecting them, is to make one class of men sceptics, and another dogmatists; till at last the accumulated flood of doubt breaks down the thin barrier of idle and unproved assertion. To enquire reverently concerning them, has no necessary tendency to alter the received body of truth, but it may teach us a lesson of no small importance, if it makes us feel to some degree the nature of our knowledge, and of our ignorance.

"If any man will do,"—that is, wills to do—"His will, he shall know of the doctrine." In these words the text expresses a directly practical truth. In matters of conduct, in spiritual as well as in ordinary life, the first condition of attaining truth lies in the will to act according to it. The doing of what is right, comes, in a general way, before the clear knowledge of the principles which determine right. We *must* act, or abstain from action; and on many subjects abstaining from action is well nigh equivalent to acting in the opposite direction. If, *looked for in its Spirit and Purpose.*

when some person calls on us to obey him as a duty, our doubts lead us to refuse him obedience, we practically deny his authority. If, when hungry, we abstain from food which is put before us, such abstinence implies a practical belief that the food is distasteful, or unwholesome, or that it is for some reason wrong to eat it. Hence arises the danger, in all practical subjects, of methods of investigation and habits of thought which imply a long suspense of judgment with regard to matters immediately before us. Doubts may hang over the distance; but still we can make progress if they leave the foreground clear. With a few firm points on which to place our feet, we can make our way over a quagmire. But if we must advance at once, we cannot account him a benefactor, who floods the ground which lies immediately before us, while he gives us a promise that it shall be dry land next year. All information as to our course is a mockery, which does not tell us in what direction we must turn our footsteps *now*.

Suppose, then, a Christian, whose will is

really set on doing his Father's work, to meet, for the first time, in a direct and unmistakeable way, with a difficulty in the Bible —a difficulty, for instance, affecting the truth of its history, or the tone of its morality, or the structure of its prophecies. The difficulty, I need scarcely say, may not be self-sought. It may have been suggested from this pulpit; it may have come in the course of regular study or of chance reading; it may have dropped in the form of a question from the lips of a child in the nursery; it may recur with increased force, in some time of deep thought and hard trial, when the child becomes a man. How is it to be met? Often by simple humility. "Lord, I am not high-minded, I have no proud looks; I do not exercise myself in great matters, which are too high for me; but I refrain my soul, and keep it low, like as a child that is weaned from its mother; yea, my soul is even as a weaned child. O Israel, trust in the Lord, from this time forth for evermore." But if, after the exercise of prayer and faith, the old difficulty recurs; if it is found working widely, *looked for in its Spirit and Purpose.*

and in widely different minds; if the teacher is asked its solution by a pupil, if the world seems calling for it—what course is proper then?

Not to devise, or to accept from an incompetent authority, a *theory* of inspiration, and to accommodate the facts to it; not to endeavour to connect, by indissoluble bonds, the point which seems doubtful with the most important truths, and then to assert that these must stand or fall together; not to lay before shrinking and conscientious minds a false yet terrible dilemma, and say, 'believe in this manner, or else believe not at all.' It is far better calmly to consider the facts of the case, as they bear upon ourselves, excluding theory as much as possible till we have investigated the facts, and using it as little as possible afterwards. Great care will of course be necessary to keep theory from creeping in. Those often theorise most boldly, who deny that they theorise at all. A theory is often implied, where it is not asserted. It may pass itself off to the unwary as a simple fact, or hide in the shadow of a negation[1]. It may be right or wrong; but in any case we ought to be aware of its existence. We should often be startled at the small amount of our real knowledge, if we perceived how much of our seeming knowledge is an assumption.

It is best, then, to look at the facts, and this, from our own natural position. This will involve its own advantages, as well as its own responsibilities and trials. That truth, which many can only regard from without, we see by its own light from within. We are born and baptised Christians, parts of that mighty whole which covers the centuries with a luminous cloud of witnesses, revealing, though only in part, the glory of Him to whom it testifies. As members of the one body, we are connected with every one and with everything in whom and on which the Spirit of Christ has wrought. Through many changes, with great and tremendous struggles, striving in the individual heart and mind, and moulding the purposes of nations, in spite of all differences of language and doctrine and

[1] Note V.

rite and communion, that Spirit is working still. From our own point of view (am I wrong in thinking it is one of the foremost?), from that, I mean, of the Church of England, we are bound, if true to the spirit of her teaching, not to restrict our hopes and wishes and interests to ourselves, but to join, as far as possible, in prayer and thought and action, with the whole congregation of Christian men dispersed throughout the world. A strange and solemn sight meets us, if we thus look out from ourselves. With a feeling of wonder, which familiarity cannot take away, we see action extending and speculation deepening, the running to and fro of many, and the increase of knowledge, and ourselves in front of the movement. A very Babel of mind and motion would this be, were there no key-note to reduce the whole to harmony, no source traceable from which the first impulse came, no common object which all this activity, if well directed, may help to further. The complexity of the problem increases as we watch and as we work. Those read the lesson of the present day very imperfectly, who see even in its physical and mechanical activity only a tendency to a rounded and systematic materialism, in action, thought, and enjoyment. We are in little danger, at any stage of social, political, or scientific development, so long as that development is real and earnest, of ultimately losing interest in those mysteries of the inner and spiritual life, which are deeper than the depths of our thought, and higher than the scope of our action. It is in the state of easy inactive living, when a man eats leisurely the fruits of the field which scarcely calls for tillage, or sleeps still more idly on the accumulated resources of a decaying and effete civilisation, that he is apt to forget entirely those obstinate questionings of the heart, to which another world alone can give the full answer. Not so, when industry is restless, and thought almost overtasked, and the wonderful events of yesterday are being forgotten among the greater wonders of to-day, and the equipoise of the civilised world is disturbed, and the nations are trembling as they are weighed in the balance of God. If men are busy with the external world, and are asserting their control over it, yet the intensity of their action leaves their minds tremulously sensitive, at times when action is suspended or impossible. If they are exploring the secrets of nature, the most apathetic enquirer can scarcely help at times touching in spirit the hem of the garment of that great Being, whom nature at once reveals and veils. Some great convulsion of our political machinery reminds us from time to time of Him who can destroy the nations which He has made. Some terrible crash of the apparatus which we have devised for our own convenience brings very close home to us, every now and then, appalling forms of death and suffering which were strange to the old experience of mankind, and which occur as the unintentional products of our own imperfect ingenuity. An advanced civilisation only brings more frequently before us, in the persons of those whom we know, the strangely intertwined perplexities of birth, and life, and death. The skill of modern science teaches us how to prevent or mitigate some forms of physical evil;

but it also teaches us how deep the sources of evil are laid in the nature of things, and has no key to unlock the mystery of a groaning and suffering creation. Nor can we accuse this age, with all its faults, of being blind to the existence of moral evil, and of making no strenuous efforts to diminish vice and sin. Indifference, far more than doubt, is an antagonist to faith—to that faith which, while it sees endless uncertainties opening up on all sides, and confesses the incapacity of man to cope with them, turns to the one Source of all the varied forms of Being, and rests and worships at the footstool of God. It is a blessing, whatever we are sometimes tempted to think, that we do not live in times when we can afford to be torpid in the midst of a torpid world, and idle, though as busy as others. It is a still greater blessing, that the position both of our Church and nation forbids us to adopt any extreme form of thought, or to believe that we have discovered some absolute middle point on which we may poise our opinions, persuading ourselves, without warrant of fact or evidence, that it is the very centre on which all truth turns, and toward which all minds gravitate. Standing where we do, looking backward and forward and upward, we are conscious of both poles of truth, and the foes neither of faith nor knowledge. As neither by fault nor merit of our own, we stand in the van of progress, we are conscious of that common voice which comes, though often in faint and broken tones, from the whole of that quarter of the world, whose impulse now rules the rest, and which alone has learned, in any degree whatsoever, to reconcile permanence of inward belief with freedom and plasticity of outward action. We rejoice, that among all diversities of race, and education, and manners, in spite of some avowed relinquishment of faith, and much conscious or unconscious indifference, one name, and one name only in common, is spoken, beside the awful name of God, whenever the heart of man seeks relief, by uttering its inner secret in the presence of its Maker. When we mourn over the dead, or pray by the dying, when love would find its choicest and most powerful expression, even when hate has lately been stronger than love amid the shout of armies and the din of battle, our love, our tenderness, our fear, our hope, our sorrow, turn instinctively for utterance to the name of Christ, who as man revealed to man that love and tenderness which are His Divine inheritance, and bore also the sufferings and sorrows and fears which by inheritance were ours.

Of Him, the Word of God, Himself God, in whom God was, reconciling the world to Himself, Christians agree to believe that there is no record like the Bible. Some, it is true, in the spirit of an older dispensation than the Christian, veil its glories from the sight of the people, and dare not entrust to themselves or others the knowledge of its plain out-spoken truths. But even these, far from depreciating the contents of the casket of which they hold the key, make its sacredness the excuse of their ill-judged reserve, and acknowledge its value in the error which restricts its use. Others, by an opposite error, at the bottom of which in many cases there may also lie a spirit of Jewish presumption or Jewish fear, assert the sufficiency of Holy Scripture, but in a sense which sounds too like an assertion of their own self-sufficiency. They say, or seem to say, that they themselves, with the assistance only of that spiritual light which God vouchsafes to all whom He loves, could, by the sole aid of its pages, and without the use of all the checks and assistances with which God has surrounded one of the most precious of His works, trace out for themselves, not only the form and outline, but the details of saving truth, make it their own, hold it firm, and teach it to others. But we need not now discuss the probable success of an experiment which, from the nature of things, never has been made, and never can be. Let us look rather at the points of agreement than at those of difference. Let us regard all Christendom, not only as believing in Christ, but as loving and cherishing His written word. What is the reason which all sects and Churches are most likely to agree in, were they asked their reason for this veneration of the Bible?

Surely, because it contains the records of a *Life*, of the conditions which preceded it, and of the consequences which followed it; because we read there the History of Him, without whose Divine Life the world was not, and without whose Human Life the Church was not. Here we approach most closely to the words of Him, who spake as never man spake; here we see, cast on our common humanity, the most direct beam of His light, who lighteth every man that cometh into the world. Here we perceive the beginning of the dispensation, which has built together human souls upon the foundation of the Apostles and Prophets, Jesus Christ Himself being the head corner-stone, in whom the whole building fitly framed together has grown, and is growing still, unto a Holy Temple in the Lord. The Temple might still exist, though we were ignorant of the foundation. We dare not restrict the working of the Spirit of God to that which the Spirit inhabits: still less should we have a right to deny the edifice to be His, because we were not allowed to know much of His method in building it. The mystery of the existing state of things would be at least as much increased as diminished, if we were left in comparative ignorance of the Divine Architect who formed the design, and of the wise master-builders who raised the structure on the foundation which He alone could lay. But we are not left in such ignorance; and that which saves us from it is the record of the New Testament Scriptures.

The New Testament, then (for of that alone we speak at present), is the record of the Life, and Death, and Work of Christ, in themselves and in their consequences. Thus much seems clear. Let us proceed to look a little more closely into the nature and formation of this record.

Nor, in speaking of its nature and formation, shall we be in any danger of going wrong, when we describe this nature and formation as designed by God. I am not ignorant (no one who has thought upon the subject can be ignorant) of the speculative difficulties which we must encounter, when we speak of the purposes of God. We cannot mention the reason or design of His works, name Him as the First Cause, or use any expression to describe His willing and working, without using language which has reference primarily to our limited human powers. But all that need be said now, is that these difficulties are in no way peculiar to our present subject. We can speak of the purpose of God as shewn in the formation of Holy Scripture, with *at least* as much propriety (to speak guardedly) as we can of His design exhibited in the petal of a flower or the wing of an insect. If the result which follows from the working of material laws may properly be ascribed to Him, the result of spiritual laws may properly be ascribed to Him likewise. One important point of distinction, no doubt, exists between the works of matter and those of mind, when viewed in reference to the Maker of both mind and matter. Merely material results, though often arising from sinful acts, and bearing the marks of sin, are not in themselves properly sinful. But when man appears as a moral agent, a new element is introduced by the possibility of abusing that mysterious power of will, of the existence of which our own conscience is the best assurance, and the abuse of which we dare not regard as in any sense a work designed by God. But to our present subject this distinction does not apply. That view, at once most false and most superficial, which regards the body of early Christian documents as the work of deliberate and intentional fraud, has passed away, probably for ever. And, the action of sin excluded, we should obviously be most rash in denying, that God, under whose guidance each material particle seeks its own appointed place, guides the working of honest human minds, when seeking for, or teaching, the truth. But we are not now considering the operation of the human mind in the formation of Holy Scripture. This alone we assume, that there was no such element of thought at work in the minds of those who wrote Holy Scripture, as should prevent us from describing those features in its structure, which clearly are not the result of any individual human mind, as being designed by God.

On the present occasion, without entering fully on a subject which I hope to pursue hereafter from this place, let me briefly call your attention to the general structure of the New Testament, in some of those broad features, which cannot be ascribed to the mind of the separate writers, and which yet we should all be very sorry not to regard as a part of its Divine organisation. About the facts there is, I believe, comparatively little difference of opinion among candid and fair judging men. Perhaps it would be rash to assume that there will be an equal agreement concerning the moral deducible from them; yet this also seems fairly clear.

When did the New Testament first pass, as a whole, before a single human mind? who first wrote, or read, or studied it, as a complete and separate volume? We know not, and we cannot know. But the work has been done, though we cannot say how or when. The date can be fixed proximately, the process traced partly by conjecture; the fact alone is certain, that its separate portions have now, through many centuries, been knit together into a closer unity than at first belonged to them. Let us see what parts go to make up the whole.

We find four lives of our Saviour, each marked by its own peculiarities. Three of the four have many obvious points of connection and similarity, recording on the whole the same portion of the life of Christ, and limiting themselves, during the greater part of their narrative, to His sojourn and works in Galilee. The resemblance between them, though broken and modified by numerous differences, is so strong and unmistakeable as to point, by general consent, to some community of origin. In some way or other, it is generally allowed, the three earlier Evangelists had access to the same materials. They saw each other's Gospels; or they had before them some earlier Gospel which is lost; or they arranged according to some special law the written fragments of the Divine life, which they found already in circulation; or they expressed, in their own manner, a uniform and received tradition common to the Apostolic college. With these suppositions, and others like them, the simple reader, who wanders unaware among them, finds himself utterly perplexed. He sees authorities at variance, each convincing himself that he is right, but seldom succeeding in convincing his brother. If he endeavours to judge between them for himself, he finds himself engaged in a task which quite transcends his powers of analysis and judgment. He has passed, perhaps without knowing it, from facts to theories. He is involved in questions, not about important truths, but about the mechanism by which these truths have been taught. From contemplating the Divine life, he has betaken himself to dissecting its history.

If from examining the structure of the Gospels he turns to enquiring about their authors, and the warrant on which he accepts their teaching, he may easily discover for himself a parallel set of difficulties. Indeed it is possible, nay, it is highly probable, that some short-sighted and one-sided teacher may place the difficulties before him, as the only solid basis on which he can build his faith.

looked for in its Spirit and Purpose. 49

He may be told that the Apostles were the appointed teachers of all Christian truth, and that he should accept the Gospels only on the authority of the Apostles: that St Matthew was an Apostle, St John was an Apostle, that St Mark was not an Apostle, but was instructed by St Peter, St Luke was not an Apostle, but records the teaching of St Paul. Many who are here present know much, though not all, that is to be said on these points. Before considering them in detail, it might be well for each of us to ponder carefully the meaning of that text—"he gave some, apostles; and some, prophets; and some, evangelists; and some, pastors and teachers; for the perfecting of the saints, for the work of the ministry, for the edifying of the body of Christ[1]." But, waiving the general principle involved, let us take the outline of the question of fact. It is not absolutely proved that St Matthew wrote the Gospel which bears his name, though we have considerable external evidence that he did, and internal evidence which confirms it, though

[1] Ephes. iv. 11, 12.

complicated, as we might expect, with some difficulties. As for St John's Gospel, in spite of the comparatively late character of its external evidence, for which it is not difficult to account, few, very few, can refuse their ready recognition of the Divine life and light stored up in that wonderful narrative, in which the spirit of love blends the vivid recollections of youth with the contemplative sweetness of old age. In the case of the two remaining gospels, external evidence declares what they do not assert themselves, that they were written by St Mark and St Luke; while the connection of St Mark with St Peter is highly probable, and that of St Luke with St Paul is indisputable. The result of enquiries like these will prove, I believe, in the long run, most satisfactory. But we shall be long in arriving at the result, in proportion as they are fairly and earnestly made. And if they are to be regarded as the basis of our faith, what is to be the poise of the soul while they are going on? How are devotion and worship possible, when we are staking their propriety on the balance of probabilities? What power has the heart to spring upward, while in a state of trembling doubt whether the ground from which it ought to spring is certain or uncertain? Was there any occasion thus to wander into the border-land of faith and doubt, that we might slowly and painfully retrace our steps to faith? When infinite truth and purity, clothed in the veil of flesh, enters our presence accompanied by four venerable forms, about which clings some of the darkness which skirts an excess of light, is it desirable that we turn from the centre of light to which they point, and demand time to examine their credentials? When of old Philip told Nathanael that he had found that Jesus of whom Moses and the Prophets wrote, and Nathanael answered with words of doubt, Philip did not reply to Nathanael by a challenge to examine his credibility as a witness, but by an invitation to come and see. Surely it is no duty of a Christian man to interpose the personality even of an Apostle between himself and his Saviour. The words of an Apostle, at least, suggest a different order:—"All things are yours, whether

Paul, or Apollos, or Cephas, or the world, or life, or death; all are yours, and ye are Christ's, and Christ is God's[1]."

Enough has probably been said on the structure and origin of the Gospels, to render unnecessary a detailed reference to the Epistles, and to those other books which we classify with them more naturally than with the Gospels. Suffice it to say, that we find in these documents a structure unlike that of the Gospels, and yet in many respects analogous. The character of St Paul, as it appears in his own Epistles, stands forward, of course, as a perpetual wonder. No other portrait of a great man has ever been brought before the world, by his own writings or another's, with such clear, forcible, and enduring vitality; as if the very man were present, rebuking, beseeching, expostulating, living, working, praying. The intense humanity of one of the world's greatest benefactors has been thus brought out so strongly, that while even the unbelieving have admired it, not even the superstitious have worshipped it. His letters

---

[1] 1 Cor. iii. 21—23.

have been indeed more powerful than his bodily presence. Through them, since his departure to Christ, he has more than once moved visibly the Christian world. He has told us much of himself, more of Christ, and yet how differently from the Gospels. "Though we have known Christ after the flesh, yet now henceforth know we Him no more[1]." The facts of the Gospel are recognised in his teaching, not simply as historical events, but as incorporated with its doctrines. The Cross of Christ in which he gloried was not that borne by Simon of Cyrene, the father of Alexander and Rufus, but that whereby the world was crucified to him and he unto the world. The same remark, though with various degrees of modification, applies to the other Epistles not written by St Paul, which are contained in the Sacred Volume. Into their several peculiarities we cannot now enter. Those who have studied the subject will remember that it is precisely that Epistle which contains the most definite allusions to its writer's intercourse with our Lord, which learned

[1] 2 Cor. v. 16.

men have found most difficulty in assigning to its supposed author[1]. But, with or without this fact, the general truth is clear. Holy Scripture discloses on examination a very varied and complex organisation. But we can often see the purpose of an instrument, and use it very effectually, without fully understanding how it is made. And surely Holy Scripture, in its general design, is an instrument, not an end. It is meant, by the assistance of the Holy Spirit, to guide our souls to Christ. Much light will be cast upon its structure by its proper use; apart from its proper use, we can scarcely expect to understand its structure.

"Now we see through a glass darkly." The glass is not the object of contemplation, but something beyond it. The telescope is well-nigh indispensable to the astronomer; yet his science deals not with it, but with the star. He indeed has often much to do with the construction of the instrument which he uses. It is made to meet his taste, and serve his peculiar purposes. He knows its nature

[1] Note VI.

too well to fall into the same errors with regard to it, which are too common with us when we speculate about that Divine instrument, which extends our sphere of vision beyond this world into the next. Rash and presumptuous that we are, often, when we are laying claim to humility, we place ourselves, while still learners, in the position of teachers, and dogmatise, when we should wait. Not content with the lawful use of the treasure committed to us, perhaps to the positive neglect of its lawful use, we employ it for other purposes, for which we have no warrant that it was intended. Because through it we see more clearly the sun, and moon, and stars; we look eagerly at the woods and fields and trees, darkly reflected on a small scale, and with some necessary disproportion, on its object-glass, and declare that there is no knowledge of the outer world like this. Because through it, with achromatic clearness, the ray of light pierces to the soul, we pronounce in our ignorance that its every lens is clear and perfect crystal, with no difference in the degree of its purity, no variation in its refractive power. Or, if we do not pronounce rashly, we stand and argue, till the star sweeps from the field and is lost: and then, happy are we if we forget ourselves and our speculations, and search diligently till we find it.

May God give us all the single eye to behold His truth, and the pure and loving heart which turns to it, as a growing plant turns towards the light. May there spring up strong within us the will to do His will, and bring with it the fuller knowledge of the doctrine. Young and old, learned and unlearned, wise and unwise, the peasant who tills the fields, the workman who toils in the factory, the minister who feeds the flock of Christ, the reader and the thinker, the teacher and the learner, can walk in *this* way together. Their courses, if not parallel, shall be convergent. Only on the other side of the dark river, can we hope all to meet on that heavenly hill, whose deep foundations are laid in the eternal Truth, and whose heights are crowned with the city of the great King. Towards Him, as He sits on his everlasting throne, loving hearts are flocking from every quarter. The holy mount itself may hide them from each other: He from its summit sees and knows them all. May all our faces be set towards Him; and if, as we seek a fuller knowledge of His truth, our progress is slow, and we have nothing fresh to tell, His love is always new. Only, let our apparent slowness be not the result of indifference, or cowardice, or idleness. It would be well indeed if the lamp of truth travelled fast; it is much more important to keep it always burning. We may well seem to be slow, when the proportions of all about us are so vast, and our every step should be careful. In all probability, no new truths await us; but we are called to know something more than we do of the length and breadth and depth and height of truths which we have learned already. As we grow to the full proportion of men, we must not expect our increase in wisdom and knowledge to be quicker than our growth (and when was that fast?) in humility, and self-denial, and love.

SERMON III.

THE DIFFICULTY OF APPROACHING THE INSPIRATION OF HOLY SCRIPTURE THROUGH THE INSPIRATION OF ITS WRITERS.

Preached at St Mary's Church, 20 May, 1860.

2 PETER I. 21.

For the prophecy came not in old time by the will of man: but holy men of God spake as they were moved by the Holy Ghost[1].

IN dealing with a subject of great extent and high importance, we may think it very advisable to devote especial attention to one of its particular aspects, and yet be far from thinking it desirable that this aspect should be allowed to exclude every other. At the present day, it may be very necessary to con-

[1] Note VII.

sider, as we have hitherto done, Holy Scripture as a whole, and as a whole designed by God as an instrument for a definite purpose; but it can be neither necessary nor possible to forget that it is made up of parts, and that each of these parts has its author. Nor should it be forgotten that part and whole are relative rather than opposed conceptions. We look at the instrument; we see that one mind has adapted its parts to a single purpose: but we also see that, to form each of these parts, subordinate agents wrought with hand and mind. God in His Providence has joined the several books together in a volume; the several books were written by individual men.

Here, of course, we must not be misled by a true yet partial antithesis. We must not simply say—the Volume is of God; the component books are of men. God wrought through unknown agents in putting the volume together. He wrought through agents, more or less known, in writing the several books. Let us avoid in this case, as in others, the practical fallacy, of attributing more or less of a work to God, in proportion as we see less or more of the secondary causes which have been employed in forming it.

"Prophecy came not of old by the will of man; but holy men of old spake, moved by the Holy Ghost." We cannot doubt that in this way the writers of the New Testament regarded the writers of the Old. We can doubt just as little that later ages have, consciously or unconsciously, transferred at once the letter and the spirit of these words to a new sphere of thought, and have looked on the writers of the New Testament Scriptures with a like reverence to that with which those writers turned to those who had gone before them, the authors of the books of the older Covenant. Happily there is no need to question any part of the process. We acknowledge that the One Spirit, who has been from the beginning, and has never ceased to work in this our earth, since first He moved on the face of the darkling waters, wrought through the Jewish institutions, and through institutions older than the Jewish, making things ready for that fulness of time when God sent forth His Son. We can sympathise fully with Apostles and Evangelists, who, standing in the light of the perfect day, looked back to earlier times, and venerated the forerunners of Apostle and Evangelist. Like them, we see in their writings much which, though written under a perishing dispensation, has reference to eternal truth; much even of local and temporal allusion, which passes on beyond its earlier limits of place and time, and meets with its consummation in Christ. Doubtless they spoke, moved by the Spirit of God; doubtless their words had a meaning independent of and beyond their will. We assent readily when we hear the New Testament teachers speaking thus of the Old Testament writers, and in assenting, by a true and natural instinct, assign the same gifts and graces, the gifts and graces of holiness and inspiration, to the writers of the New Testament, which they assigned to the writers of the Old. Of many of the writers of the Old Testament, as individuals, we know little or nothing; but we know that they helped to do God's work, and we believe that they did so by the Spirit of God. Much more do we believe this of the writers of the New Testament, even in cases when we cannot determine with certainty who they are. No gift or grace would we deny them which the facts of the case allow us to grant. Along with all ages we wish to assign, in Christian reverence and love, the fullest spiritual privileges to those who come so very close to Christ. Sinlessness and unerring perfection, indeed, we must not attribute to them, because their own writings disclaim them. And great as is the interval in time, in circumstance, in spirit, which parts them from the Old Testament writers, we feel a unity between the two groups of authors, because they are one in Christ. From our point of view, far along the ages, the point at which the New Testament emerges has become old as a matter of history, and the two clusters of figures almost melt into one. Apostle and Evangelist believe that Prophet and Psalmist spoke as they were moved by the Holy Ghost. We take the words spoken of Prophet and Psalmist, and apply them in a still higher sense to

Apostle and Evangelist. There was a time when among those born of women there had not risen a greater than John the Baptist; but he that is least in the kingdom of Heaven is greater than he.

And here, if we adopted the ordinary mode of treating the subject, would come in at once a vast and overwhelming army of questions—perplexed, abstruse, difficult, and yet requiring to be settled one way or the other, before the devout yet intelligent Christian can properly read his Bible. Who that really knows at all the awful depth and mystery of the subject, does not shrink from supposing that he is called upon, or may call on others, at some early stage of the Christian life, to settle, as a condition of the profitable study of Holy Scripture, the principal questions which concern the nature and degrees of Inspiration? Let us put the problem in other words, and regard it for a moment. There have lived, during a period of three thousand years, more or less, a series of writers. They had this feature in common, that they were all teachers of a progressive system, not acting according to their own wills only, or knowing precisely the place of their teaching as relative to the system which they helped to further. Sometimes they recorded the past, sometimes they dwelt upon the present, sometimes they anticipated the future, sometimes they insisted on those great moral truths which belong to all time and to eternity. They are authors, or compilers, or arrangers; quoters of other books, stringers together of sweet songs by many hands. Their names, their dates, their characters, are to a great degree unknown. We wish to study their works in their living relation to a great living and moving system. We are called upon to suspend, if not the study, at least its most precious practical results, till we can, in our knowledge, or our ignorance, give some comprehensive expression of the mental and spiritual state, in which all of these, Jew and Christian, known and unknown, historian, prophet, psalmist, evangelist, apostle; writer, dictator, arranger, must be supposed all alike to have been when they composed their books.

"They were inspired." Yes; we freely

as approached through its Writers. 65

grant it. The organs of the Divine mind, the instruments of the Divine purpose, the messengers of the Divine will, the teachers of spiritual truth, the builders and, under Christ, the founders of a spiritual system, the fathers of that spiritual society to which the Holy Spirit is the very breath of life, the writers of inspired Scripture, they were undoubtedly inspired. "They were guided by God;" true; and we also, guided by God in our measure, if we do not, like deaf adders, stop our ears, and are not indifferent of set purpose to any form of His teaching, may read their writings as the words of those who, through the long course of ages, have heard the guiding voice, and felt the guiding hand, nay, who have been, some of them, marvellously and unspeakably close to Him who was from the beginning, whom they had heard, whom they had seen with their eyes, whom they had looked upon, and their hands had handled, of the Word of life. But in this there is no theory; or at least no theory narrower or more definite than the great fact of Christianity, than the Church and the Gospel; only a sense, however expressed, or not expressed at all, that the mystery of Being and of thought becomes deeper as it approaches closer to that Divine Person on whom our love and hopes are set. What a vast leap from this point to theories of dynamical or mechanical inspiration, to technical distinctions between revelation and inspiration, to questions of infallibility and degrees of inspiration, to speculations about direction and suggestion, and illumination, and dictation, and all the array of self-chosen terminology, which is employed in the endeavour to match an hypothesis to the facts of the case, and to measure a mystery by our imperfect knowledge. How far are we still, and happily, from that summary method, which first hardens the letter of Holy Scripture to a dead uniformity, and then applies to it the mailed hand of logical argument, to force a meaning from it; not touching it carefully and handling it reverently, as if it were a feeling and living thing. Surely, if on any subject we should beware of easy solutions and hasty conclusions, it is on this. The Church Universal has ruled little or nothing concerning it. Our own

Communion is nearly silent upon it[1]. She sends us, indeed, to the deep and living well; she bids us draw, and tells us that in spite of its depth, we *can* draw; she tells us to regard it as a heritage from our forefathers; she shews us Christ sitting by it. And yet, we shall follow neither her guidance, nor His, if, turning from essential truths, and pausing in the work of life, we take to asking curious questions—questions, not of direct practical import, but pointing to controversies which are not of godliness, and differences between the Churches—quite forgetting, while we argue or are curious about them, the causes which perhaps have gendered or intensified them—our sins and the sins of our fathers.

In declining therefore, and requesting others to consider whether they should not decline, that method of investigation, which will not allow us to accept the Bible as the Word of God, without technical theories as to the mental state in which His Messengers delivered it, let me call your attention, in the same connection, to another important circum-

[1] Note VIII.

stance. All these subjective theories, if made in any way the basis of our treatment of Holy Scripture, are liable to a grave objection not yet hinted at, and of quite a different nature. At first sight, they recommend themselves by their air of soundness and completeness. Although, in all probability, merely temporary hypotheses, which we employ to arrange our opinions and our knowledge, and which we modify, consciously or unconsciously, from time to time, to correspond with their variations, their systematic form tempts us by an offer of security. Here, it seems, we can pause; on this basis we can take our stand; for this reason we can believe. And no doubt, if simple intellectual consistency, apart both from fact, and from the moral necessities of our nature, were the test of religious truth, we could best hope to attain it by some device of this kind. In that case, the further apart it was from all that was divine and mysterious, the more purely independent of all our spiritual experience, the better. It is easy to construct a system which shall be in some sense necessarily true, if we are at liberty to begin by assuming premises which can neither be proved nor disproved, and to decline all appeal to fact and experience at the end. But happily no one would wish to discover a theoretical perfection of this kind in religious truth. Most persons would at once acknowledge, that they needed less a Gospel consistent and coherent in itself, than one which should give a coherency to things and ideas which are in their nature disposed to separate, and should knit together, by the bonds of hope and faith and love, life and death, this world and the next, God and man, man and his brethren. For this purpose, theories such as we have mentioned are by themselves wholly insufficient. To make them bear upon the spiritual life, they require additions which seem to supersede their necessity. With all their show of completeness, it will, I believe, appear that they are, for more than one reason, inoperative.

And first, as regards the letter of Holy Scripture. Between it, and any theory about the spiritual state of its writers, there lies an important interval. Had we the most absolute certainty that, as they wrote it, its every word and letter was unchangeable truth and perfection, it will not follow that we can say as much of it, as we read it. We have no sufficient reason to believe that we read in every case exactly what they wrote; and much reason to believe the contrary. Let us remember some of the facts, as they concern the New Testament. The close of St Mark's Gospel is, it is now generally admitted, written by another hand. There are two passages in St John's Gospel, one describing the particulars of a miracle, the other narrating a Divine act of mercy, which judicious criticism is slow to receive[1]. The famous passage about the three heavenly witnesses, though it still stands in the services of our Church, is now generally surrendered; and a textual uncertainty, not I believe without a very significant and precious meaning, hangs about several important texts which bear upon the Divinity of our blessed Lord[2]. With regard to the whole Gospel of St Matthew, it is not yet decided whether we receive it in the original,

[1] Note IX.   [2] Note X.

or as a translation; and those who know anything about translations are aware of the importance of the point in question. It should not be forgotten that Holy Scripture is, to the immense majority of its readers, *wholly* a translation, in which of course not one word occurs exactly as it was first written. It may be added, that all but thoroughly practised scholars, when they consult the Greek Testament in the original, though they read in Greek, think in English, and thus in fact translate for themselves, and are liable to all the errors of translators. Thus then stand the facts. After three centuries, at the least, of oral tradition and transcription, we see at length a text of the sacred books begin to emerge. Its general fidelity is unshaken; but we cannot doubt that here and there alterations have been made, even in important passages. We do not read exactly what the authors wrote. Some changes have been made in that veil of words, through which mind discourses with mind.

But to all this an answer at once occurs to the fair and candid thinker. We shrink instinctively from any view which stakes great and enduring interests simply on verbal and textual criticism. Surely, it strikes us, these documents, so old and venerable, for so many centuries the care of Christendom, read prayerfully, transcribed carefully, preserved diligently, are not corrupt and untrustworthy, like salt which has lost its savour. Through three or four centuries, during which we cannot accurately trace their text, their Divine author doubtless guarded them, that they might move a long chain of centuries afterwards. Are we to think that transcribers and translators have done unintentional harm to the cause which they wished to serve, and have hidden the burning lamp of truth in their mistaken caution, or have well nigh extinguished it in their careless haste to pass it on from hand to hand ? Is not the very contrary the better and the truer supposition ? If we retain, and are content to retain certain passages in our Bibles, which we have reason to believe are alterations or insertions, has not this conduct its moral ? We must not make it an excuse, indeed, for any unfairness and disingenuousness. We must acknowledge on due occasion, what the facts of the case are, and freely admit that there may be similar cases, few or many, where we cannot trace them, and it may be do not suspect them. But may we not still rest in the hope that meanwhile God, while committing His truth to human and fallible means, has not ceased to care for it, that the laws of transmission which modify it do not destroy it, and the very cloud which covers it is luminous with an undying light, because the Sun is behind it?

A most true, I believe, and a most happy hope. But in what lies its cheering virtue? Is it not in this—that while it recognises the Spirit of God as working, in an especial sense, with the first authors of Holy Writ, it recognises also the Providence of God as directing its subsequent history? It robs the distant past of nothing; but it also glorifies the present. It allows us to see a moral in doubt, and a meaning in obscurity. It bids us look, with a real though discriminating reverence, not only on the sacred Word, and on the pillar on which God has graven it, but also, provided they do not obscure the inscription, on every moss and lichen which has grown upon it, every tint which the course of ages has added to its surface. Let us take an extreme instance—the narrative of the woman taken in adultery. Critics in general, of very different schools, are agreed that it is, in the strictest and narrowest sense of the term, no part of St John's Gospel. Are we prepared therefore simply to eject it from our Bibles? Do we regard it with a holy indignation, as an unlawful addition to the Word of God? Would we have it forgotten entirely, or relegated to some Codex Apocryphus? Would the lacuna which its absence would make be more grateful than its presence? Nay, it has rested on the rock, instinct with primitive fire, till its character is metamorphosed. We treasure it as a holy treasure, knowing that if it comes not from the Spirit of St John, it is one with the Spirit of the Bible.

These remarks, it will be seen, whatever they are worth, apply to any theory of inspiration whatever. For they amount practically to this. We cannot escape from the effect of modifying though minor changes, either upon the past, or upon ourselves. We cannot expect to look into the law which regulated the workings of holy minds in ages long gone by, with a minuteness and a certainty which we feel to be impossible in the case of the friend of our bosom. We know them through their writings, and through the consequences of those writings, or rather the consequences of that great event of which those writings testify. Those writings are changed in part, though not, we believe, essentially: the consequences of the Gospel, in connection with which we view those writings, vary with each succeeding age; we ourselves vary more or less as we look, and the change of the changing eye colours the landscape. This inevitable degree of uncertainty is not fatal to any theory; but only to its assertion as necessary for a just and profitable, though it may be partial, appreciation of the facts. It will not allow us to insist on any theory as supplying the principle of cohesion to Holy Scripture, as if the whole would break into fragments, like a

Rupert's drop, were the minutest portion displaced. But it leaves us free to decline investigations to which we are not equal, and warns us, if we must theorise, to theorise humbly and carefully, knowing that the facts are God's, and the theories are ours.

The foregoing argument, it will be seen, turns on the letter of Holy Scripture. It has been urged, in order to shew that no theory about the inspiration of the writers of Holy Writ is sufficient for practical purposes, unless it is taken in conjunction with other considerations which destroy its theoretical completeness, and deduct from its practical necessity. It may be sufficient in quitting the subject, to call attention to another argument, pointing to the same conclusion, and drawn, not from the letter, but from the Spirit.

Let us suppose, for the time, an absolutely perfect text of the New Testament, a text, that is, existing exactly as the original authors wrote it. Let us suppose further, such a full and absolute gift of the Spirit of God to the writers, that their every word should be absolutely and beyond all question indisputable. These extreme hypotheses would not suffice to enable an ordinary Christian to read his Bible profitably for his soul's health, unless he made additions to them which rendered them unnecessary. This may perhaps most easily be made obvious by an example.

Among the many marked features of the Epistles of St Paul, none stands more prominent than his repeated and energetic protests against Judaism. In no place does he state these in stronger language than in his Epistle to the Galatians. "O foolish Galatians, who hath bewitched you, that ye should not obey the truth?" "How turn ye again to the weak and beggarly elements, whereunto ye desire to be again in bondage?" "If ye be circumcised, Christ shall profit you nothing." "Christ is become of no effect unto you, whosoever of you are justified by the law, ye are fallen from grace." So spoke the Spirit to the Galatians. An important truth, no doubt; but mainly important to us for this reason, that through those words, once addressed to the Galatians, He also speaks to us. And yet the words do not apply to us directly. Christians in general do not imagine themselves bound to the observance of the Jewish Law. Circumcision is not a practice to which men are now tempted. How is it our right, why is it our duty, to take St Paul's teaching on this point to ourselves? Let it be observed, we are not denying the existence of a Judaising tendency in the Church at present. It certainly has existed widely since the times of the Apostle; it may prevail, in forms more or less obvious, among ourselves. But it does not exist in the same form which it assumed among the Galatians. What power have we of detecting it in its disguise?

It will scarcely be said that in this case, or in like cases, the faculty which we employ when we adapt Holy Scripture to circumstances which its first writer had not before his mind, is purely intellectual or logical. A real insight into the nature of the case would surely be necessary to determine what customs or opinions among ourselves stood to us in the same relation as the Jewish law to the Galatians. Here then is an occasion for moral and spiritual discernment, for comparing spiritual things with spiritual—a task, as St Paul informs us, beyond the powers of the natural man.

It would of course be idle to disguise the abuses which have resulted from the assertion of spiritual discernment, or the disputes as to those who have the right or the power of exercising it. But here, as elsewhere, the abuse must not stand in the way of the use; and the rival claims, on behalf of the Church and the individual, to the gift of spiritual insight, have often been urged in forgetfulness of the true and necessary relation in which Church and individual stand to each other. On few subjects is it more important to resist that tendency to a false antithesis—that opposition of science falsely so called—which intrudes continually into a partial Theology. The many members make the one body; and we cannot distinguish between the operation of all the members and of the whole body. Each has his share in the Divine work, without being independent of the rest. The danger of the individual lies not in his claiming his privilege, but in his asserting his independence. "I have no need of thee." We are members one of another, in connection with the one head, Christ.

It is of course true, that as some systems unduly depress the individual, others unduly exalt him. There are communities of Christians, among whom, in their corporate capacity, there is next to nothing of Christian communion. With them, isolation of spirit, except at periods of violent and unnatural excitement, seems made the law of individual development; a scanty and defective ritual banishes from the Church, on most occasions, the expression of those brotherly feelings which make us one in love; while public teaching is far more prominent than public prayer, and the emotions, which are denied their due embodiment in the Church, expand abnormally in the closet.

It is in churches such as these, for the most part, that we find separate minds growing up by themselves in strong yet morbid power, claiming Christian liberty, and identifying liberty with license; wielding the sword of the Spirit (and often the sword of the flesh as well), as if the weapon by prescriptive right were theirs, and theirs alone; and, as they read the Word of God by no other light than the light within themselves, assuming the attitude of inspired prophets interpreting inspired oracles.

"But ye have not so learned Christ." It has not been the lot of the Church of England even to be tempted to such a doubtful simplicity. Her elaborate polity, her many historical associations, her relation to complicated interests, her liturgy, gathered from sources old and new, forbid her educated and intelligent members thus to sacrifice wholly the corporate to the individual idea[1]. Still, we recognise the gift, while we believe in its wide distribution; we feel that we breathe the atmosphere of grace, though we dare not make our individual selves its centre. The Spirit of Christ, we believe, still rests upon his Church and its members. He has not so withdrawn from His people as to throw them of neces-

[1] Note XI.

sity on a broken and discontinuous Christianity. He has always remained in a real though not a localised connection, as with His sacraments, so with the Word which He first inspired. Even now there is an analogy of the faith, which may lead true hearts, following Divine guidance and the present gift of the Spirit, to many meanings of Holy Writ, which its writers did not know of.

This amounts, in fact, only to saying that educated persons may use Holy Scripture, consciously, as the most humble cottager often uses it unconsciously and well. We may take a promise from the old dispensation, and give it a meaning which belongs to the new. We may use the words which the Psalmist spoke of his own sins and sorrows, and apply them to our own. We may generalise a principle from the form in which it was first applied, and then apply it again. We may, we should, make rebukes as well as promises personal. While we do not know exactly how to interpret the language of St Paul to the Galatians, we may still find in it a present warning of God to ourselves.

One word may be added in conclusion to avoid a possible misunderstanding. Nothing can be further from my meaning, than to discourage those who have the power, from carefully and closely investigating what the language of Holy Scripture actually meant in the minds of those who wrote it. An accurate knowledge of the letter, and, when this is possible, of the circumstances under which it was written, is, in pious hands, one of the best keys to the Spirit. It is not indeed, as we all allow in the case of the utterly unlearned, indispensable to a holy life. The great moral truths which lie at the basis of religion—self-denial, and expansive love, and strict and solemn justice, may best be learned, where the world first found them in their fulness, at the very foot of the Cross. But, if we wish to know more of the laws under which the unchanging truth is seen in changing shapes, and how a lower form of teaching perishes, that a higher may rise out of it, we shall find our best lesson in the life, and writings, and character of him, whose conversion was so sudden, so wonderful, and so powerful. There we may see, in many varied lights, that freedom of spirit which springs from a holy simplicity of purpose, and that strength of will which is never so strong as when it is raised into faith; an intense love of truth coupled with an intense love of the brethren; and, among all the struggles of an eventful life, and the wrecks of a perishing dispensation, a sure and abiding reliance on the love of His Master and ours.

SERMON IV.

THE SHADOW OF THE LAW DETERMINED BY THE SUBSTANCE OF THE GOSPEL.

Preached in Christ Church Cathedral, 21 Oct. 1860.

COLOSSIANS II. 17.

Which are a shadow of things to come; but the body is of Christ.

IT has been the object of several previous discourses from this place, to show the manner in which the ordinary Christian mind can and does attain, through means appointed by God, to truths and realities which are ends rather than means. The means are precious, but the ends more precious still. The Bible is precious: but rob it, if you can in idea, of the spirit, and leave but the letter; divorce it from its relation to Christ, who gives it its fulness, and to the human soul, to which it helps to reveal the saving truth of Christ; and it will remain something very strange and wonderful, but it will have lost its blessing, and be changed into an enigma. Far from being a key to the solution of our doubts and difficulties, it will be but a fresh difficulty itself, a new perplexity in this dark and tangled world. The Church is precious; who will speak except with reverence of the bride of Christ? Christ "gave himself for her, that He might sanctify and cleanse her with the washing of water by the word, that He might present her to Himself a glorious Church, not having spot, or wrinkle, or any such thing; but that she should be holy and without blemish[1]." But make the bride a queen, apart from the right of the Bridegroom; and the mild and gentle queen becomes a cruel tyrant, tyrannising over the bodies and souls of men. She collects about her traditions, which are not after His law; she snatches at the temporal sceptre, and declares it inseparable from the spiritual. She

[1] Eph. v. 25—27.

locks up the king's volume, wherein is written the perfect law of liberty, and will neither read it herself, nor let others read it. She can persecute, or, if she can no longer persecute, she can threaten still. Her voice is not sweet and gently varied, the collective music of all Christian hearts, blended in a true, though often unpremeditated harmony, as they answer in plaintive or rejoicing strains to the Spirit of the Lord which sweeps over them. It becomes the cry of enraged and hardened men, a dry clatter of creeds and canons and articles, forced into harsh and unnatural unison, with negation for their matter and anathemas for their emphasis, among which can scarcely be heard the cry of Christ's little ones, or, if it can be heard at all, sounds by comparison faint and tremulous and untrue. So again with the ordinary providences of God. View them without an antecedent regard to the soul of man and to his Maker, and we see nothing but a blind inexorable law, tossing to and fro upon the troubled waves of being, that poor collection of atoms which we call a man, like other material beings, the sport of powers which it can neither influence nor control, though unlike them in this, that he has the supreme misery of knowing it. But all this is changed to him, who looking upon the mysteries which are placed above and below and around him, looks through them also. He exercises the primal act of Faith, and comes to God, believing that He is, and that He is the rewarder of them that diligently seek Him. He turns to God instinctively before he can turn to Him rationally, and feels after the Lord, that he may find Him. There is that within him which makes him look and listen for an answer to his spirit from without. God, he knows, is never far from him. In the strangest and darkest providence he can see at times, though sight may often fail him and faith alone remain, a trace of personal guidance. A guide, more close and more personal, he finds in the Church. His conception of it may vary greatly. He may confine it practically to a nation, or a communion, or even to a town or a parish; nay, he may narrow it, in a mistaken zeal, to the limits of some school or party with which he has come in contact, or, forgetting the injunction to call no man master, may allow an individual to exercise that authority over him which belongs to no one man, but to the collective voice of the brethren. Still, he will probably not go dangerously wrong, if, in the spirit of his Lord's command, he chooses, out of those with whom God has brought him into contact, as his guides, his fellow-thinkers, and his fellow-actors, those whom he perceives to be bringing forth, out of an honest and good heart, the peaceable fruits of righteousness. In them he sees reflected truly, though faintly and changeably, some of the lineaments of Christ. Would he see those lineaments more distinctly? We at least should know where to look for them. We seek not to build new tabernacles; for a divine Presence is in our temples even now. The Spirit of Christ is present, wherever His holy Word is read in the congregation to believing hearts which echo it. Nay, each heart is a temple. A solitary disciple now can climb the mount of transfiguration. He who reads in his chamber can catch the words which fell from the Divine Wisdom more clearly perhaps than if he had listened to them among the disciples on the mount, or heard them as they blended with the ripple of the sea of Galilee. Or has the sad hour of the Cross gone by, and the Saviour departed into heaven? Still he can watch the small band of disciples, as they labour in the name of their Lord and gather the Church about them. He can see the Apostles preaching, praying, working wonders, holding council, differing, debating, nay, for no man is perfect, contending with and rebuking each other. He knows the secret of their success; for, as they walk through the fires of a disbelieving and persecuting world, he sees Another walking with them; and His form is that of the Son of God.

It is no part of the subject which I have proposed to myself either to impugn or to assert the existence of a spiritual sense. Both in the things of time and in those of eternity, it is of much more importance to see, than to understand the manner of seeing. Almost from the time when philosophy began, the theory of vision has been a favourite subject on which metaphysician and physiologist alike might test their skill and exercise their ingenuity. A real and deep interest, of course, has lain at the bottom of these investigations. By scrutinising the nature of a single sense, and examining its organ, men have hoped to solve in part the hitherto insoluble problem, and to gain some assurance of the nature and groundwork of our knowledge. But all the time, while philosophers have been arguing and inquiring, till knowledge, and sight, and being itself, seem to disappear in a dim infinity of doubt, and mind and matter alike are volatilised in the crucible of mental analysis, ordinary men (nay even the philosophers themselves, viewed on their human and usually their better side) have been seeing, knowing, loving, hating, believing, acting. No speculations whatever have had force enough to keep their souls from stretching outwards beyond the limits of their own individuality. They have seen and known their fellow-creatures, and have rejoiced to enter into various relations with them, which are among the choicest gifts of this life, and which they delight to believe will endure into the next. Life is a reality, their life and that of others; and their knowledge is real too. The unconscious struggle of antagonist forces may be a condition of their conscious life; the unconscious harmony of many impressions may be the condition of their conscious vision; the unconscious balance of many faculties may be the condition of their conscious knowledge. But what of that? They live, and see, and know. Does any one endeavour to take the doubts which beset the theory of perception, and use them as a means of shaking their belief in the real existence of a person whom they love, or in their knowledge of that person? They will resent the endeavour with an indignation, which is wrong only if it is bitter. A man's eyes may be dim, and yet he can see his friend; he may be deaf, even to occasional misunderstanding of words, and yet he can hear and answer; time and space and personality may baffle all his attempts to understand them, and yet he knows who it was whom he met, and with whom he held sweet converse at twelve o'clock yesterday; prejudice, and passion, and weakness, and despondency may tempt and sadden him from time to time, yet through their dark and shifting mist he knows that there is love which meets his love, and a heart which answers to his heart. Try to argue him out of this belief; and he will have little patience with a destructive psychology, which would reduce all truth and all falsehood to the same dead level of despair.

And may not something of the same kind hold good in our spiritual life? Is there not here, also, a due subordination of means to ends? May it not be, in part, the trial of our faith and love, to keep our eyes and hearts fixed upon the real object of our life, while we work towards Him through means which we imperfectly comprehend, and employ a process which we cannot analyse? Is it necessary that, as children of our Heavenly Father, we should understand all the details of that complicated system of education, whereby he would lead the world, as he has millions upon millions of believing hearts already, to the saving knowledge of His Son? Are not the facts which we learn by looking through Holy Scripture, far more important than the theories which we devise from looking on it? The direct reading of Holy Scripture is, undoubtedly, not the only means by which souls have been brought to Christ. There have been many good Christians, doubtless, in days when few could read. Nay, as has been before observed, there were Christians before there were any New Testament Scriptures; an unwritten, before a written, Gospel. Still, our position with regard to Holy Scripture is unaffected by these facts, though they may make us slow to dogmatise on its exact relations to the inner life of others. To us, it is the living picture of the Divine life, the choicest treasury of Divine truth, the record of sacred Wisdom. Has any one derived from it his best and dearest assistance in his struggle against sin? Has it enabled him to realise, with a clearness and intensity denied to all other means, the person and the work of his Redeemer? Has he through it held converse with Apostles and apostolic men, till his spirit is one with theirs? Have its promises strengthened him, and its warnings quickened him to exertion? Has he found it "quick, and powerful, and sharper than any two-edged sword, piercing even to the dividing asunder of soul and spirit, and of the joints and marrow, and discerner of the thoughts and intents of the heart[1]"? Strange expressions indeed were these to use of the written word, were not the Incarnate Word, who is a quickening Spirit, at once veiled and revealed by it. Neither its letter nor its meaning may be always certain; some doubt there may be as to the writers of particular books; Apostles, standing on the edge of the old and new dispensation, may not exactly coincide in the tone of their teaching; variations may be found in the narratives of the Evangelists: still, through the written Word, by means of something above the letter, the believer sees his Saviour.

And may not this view of the Inspiration of Holy Scripture suffice for the needs of at least some of us, as we walk for a few short

[1] Heb. iv. 12.

years the ways of this troublesome world? It calls for no long period of suspense. It begins with no destructive process. It implies no unhealthy isolation of the individual mind. It invites to a free and practical recognition of God's Providence, in His dealings with the Church and the World. It leaves many difficulties unsolved; but it does not leave them lying like a wall up-piled around the truth, and forming a barrier between the soul and God. It allows, nay, it encourages, enquiry upon a basis of faith. It has its postulates, as every view must have, which aims, however feebly and imperfectly, at connecting truth with truth. But those postulates are less intellectual than spiritual and moral. It is no unworthy assumption to begin by believing that God is our teacher, in His Providence, His Church, and His Word.

Hitherto, throughout this discourse and those which have preceded it, our remarks have been confined to the structure of the New Testament. Little mention has been made of the Scriptures of the Old Covenant. Nor does it seem that the procedure could

determined by the Substance of the Gospel. 97

with propriety have been reversed. It is better to proceed from that which is near to us, to that which is further off. But the same principles probably apply to the Old Testament, which have already been applied to the New. Their application in detail to the writings of the earlier covenant is indeed far more difficult, but happily it is also less necessary. We may move with comparative safety among the shadows of the law, if we keep our hold on the body, which is of Christ.

Our providential position with regard to the Scriptures of the Old Testament, taken by themselves, is marked and peculiar. We view them from without, and not from within. They belong to a dispensation which has passed away. The ministration to which they appertained was glorious; but still it was a "ministration of death[1]." But "Jesus Christ has abolished death, and brought life and immortality to light through the Gospel[2]." "The law was given by Moses, but grace and truth came by Jesus Christ[3]."

[1] 2 Cor. iii. 7. [2] 2 Tim. i. 10. [3] John i. 17.

Now, if there is any validity in the line of argument which we have hitherto pursued, we should, as a matter of duty, if we would walk in the path which God has chosen for us, and not choose our own, approach the Old Testament from an actual and not an ideal position. We must not, even in idea, put ourselves in the position of Jews; but constantly remember that we are Christians. We are false to our position if for a single moment we make the Gospel depend upon the law.

We not unfrequently meet with the expression, that the Gospel is founded upon the law. But such language is neither according to the letter nor the spirit of Holy Scripture. "Other foundation can no man lay than that is laid, which is Jesus Christ[1]." The house of God is "built upon the foundation of the Apostles and Prophets, Jesus Christ Himself being the chief corner-stone[2]." The foundation necessarily coexists with that which is built upon it; and the prophetic and Apostolic teaching coexists with the teaching, and work,

[1] 1 Cor. iii. 11.   [2] Eph. ii. 20.

determined by the Substance of the Gospel. 99

and Church of Christ. But this is not the relation of the Old and New Covenants. "In that he saith, A new covenant, he hath made the first old. Now that which decayeth and waxeth old is ready to vanish away[1]."

Again, it should be borne in mind that the Scriptures of the Old Testament, taken by themselves, do not come to us recommended by any external authority. Once there was a society, invested with Divine sanctions, with which they had an organic connection; but that society has passed away. The scattered remnants of the old Jewish Church have many claims on our interest and pity, but none on our allegiance. It is not so with the Scriptures of the New Testament. They have, as we have seen, an organic and structural connection with a great society, still existing, of which we are members, and which has strong claims on our allegiance, the Church of Christ.

It is then as already Christians we should approach the law; it is from the ministration of life that we should look back on that of

[1] Heb. viii. 13.

death ; it is through the Scriptures of the New Covenant that we should view those of the Old. In this respect, the position in which God has placed us differs most importantly from that in which He placed those who were first called upon to receive the Gospel. Theirs was the order of learning, as ours is that of knowledge. Christ called the heathen into His Kingdom from the region of outer darkness ; He called the Jews from a region of imperfect light. The law was a schoolmaster to bring them to Christ. The volume of the law, which they held in their hands, was luminous while in the darkness; in the light, it has itself become dark—a shadow cast backward into the ages by "the true Light which lighteth every man that cometh into the world."

Accordingly, the attentive student of Holy Scripture will find something very remarkable in the manner in which the Old Testament is introduced in the New. It is rather claimed as a witness than appealed to as an authority. Our Lord, who continually employs its witness to His Divine mission and character, still places Himself above it. He confutes by its means the unworthy refinements of the scribes and Pharisees with regard to the Sabbath-day: yet with respect even to this most ancient and venerable institution of the law, His closing words are—"the Son of Man is Lord also of the Sabbath[1]." St Paul, who uses that strong and powerful language, which we know so well, regarding the inspiration and utility of the Old Testament, declares himself also an able minister "not of the letter, but of the spirit: for the letter killeth, but the spirit giveth life[2]." And surely all of us, who have reverently and carefully, with the use of ordinary apparatus, studied the quotations from the Old Testament which occur in the New, must have been, for the time at least, surprised at the result which met our enquiries. How strange seem many of these applications of things old to new; how far from exact as quotations, how abruptly divorced from their context. The difficulty would indeed be great, perhaps insuperable, if we were bound to regard these and other passages of the Old

[1] Mark ii. 28.   [2] 2 Cor. iii. 6.

Testament, as supplying the matter out of which the New Testament was made; as logical premises, including of necessity the sublime conclusions of the Gospel; as foundations deeply and strongly laid, to support the fabric to be built upon them. Of course we are not so bound to regard them; we are rather forbidden to do so. The law and its documents suggest, reflect, anticipate, imply by analogy, but do not contain the Gospel. The salient lights upon its surface were but reflections from a higher and purer light. "Beginning at Moses and all the prophets," the risen Saviour expounded to the disciples "the things concerning Himself[1]." Their hearts burned within them, while He talked with them by the way, and while He opened to them the Scriptures[2]. Their eyes were opened, and they knew Him. How little of that teaching remains for us! How comparatively few and obscure are the places of the Old Testament Scriptures to which Christ and His Apostles appeal! How often, when they are appealed to, do we find them taken from their original

---

[1] Luke xxiv. 27. [2] v. 32.

sense, and employed in some new meaning! But of this we know the history. The Author and Finisher of our Faith then stood upon the earth over against, nay in a sense within, the Old Dispensation. No wonder that His presence brought out in full relief a thousand deep and hidden meanings which we cannot recall in His absence. Even Apostles and Evangelists have not been allowed to record much of His teaching on this point. No doubt, indeed, He taught as none could teach but Himself. The dimmest types were clearly seen in the presence of the great Antitype. The faintest and most irregular shadows had their meaning made visible by Him in whom dwelt all the fulness of the Godhead bodily. Perhaps too some peculiar spiritual gift, answering to their peculiar spiritual wants, was then granted to the faithful among the chosen people. An "old and constant opinion," not wholly human though clearly observable by man, opened discerning eyes to the indications of the Messiah. A deep prophetic sympathy, like that which we attribute to dying men, may have worked in faithful hearts at the crisis of a dying dispensation[1]. Be that as it may; that state of things is gone for ever. Our Lord has departed; but He has left the Comforter behind Him. The glory of the Old Testament has waxed faint before the later formation and greater illumination of the New. The Law has expired after giving birth to the Gospel. A veil is still on its face, that veil which of old faithful eyes could penetrate, when looking towards Christ; but the same obstacle which could not prevent the eye from looking from darkness into light, may prevent the eye from looking from light into darkness. The chosen people is dispersed: the temple is destroyed; the sacrifice completed and abolished. The ceremonial is gone; the moral law indefinitely elevated and expanded by the life and words of Him who spoke with authority upon a mount which was not the hill of Sinai. When so much of the dispensation has been withdrawn into distance and darkness, can we be surprised if some obscurity and uncertainty rest upon its history?

[1] Note XII.

determined by the Substance of the Gospel. 105

The most obvious and the most practical sanction of that history is moral rather than intellectual. It lies in its close connection with the history of the Gospel. We receive it willingly, because it comes so near to Christ. Its general truth appears to be presupposed in the whole Gospel narrative, as well as in the arguments of the Epistles. Remove it; and the back-ground of thought, in front of which the Divine figure moves, is gone. The Pharisees and Sadducees still throng around Him; the Apostles and the people are there; His mother and His brethren are near Him; but where is David, His ancestor after the flesh? where is Moses, the legislator of the earlier covenant? where Abraham, the father of the faithful, and the other patriarchal forms which we see dimly through the Law, and beyond it? In like manner we are naturally attracted and influenced by every analogy which we can trace between the narrative of the Old Testament and the New. For instance, our literal belief in our Lord's resurrection makes us indisposed to take any but a literal view of the narrative of Jonah. And generally the Old Testament miracles derive a strong hold upon our faith from their resemblance to the mighty works done by Him, of whom, when we remember who He was, it may be said that in one sense His miracles are no marvel. This at least seems to be the history of the belief of the Church on the subject; and the belief of the Church, as a rule, determines that of the individual. The worship of the Church came from that of the synagogue, in the course of which the Old Testament Scriptures were read[1]. By the side of these, it would seem, was gradually formed the canon of the New Testament, till it rose in importance and dignity above them. But the Old Scriptures, though superseded in their highest function, were not removed. In spite of the energetic protest of certain parties in the early Church[2], the sense of continuity prevailed over that of difference. Hence the present structure of our Bibles. No doubt great weight is due to this, as to other providential ordinances of God. The sanction thus derived to the history of the Old Testament

[1] Note XIII.   [2] Note XIV.

determined by the Substance of the Gospel. 107

leads us in the right direction, by reminding us that the body is of Christ, and the law is the shadow.

But while we freely admit the strong presumption in favour of the Old Testament history derived from its use in the New Testament, we are also bound fairly to consider whether this argument may not be pressed too far. Let us gladly allow that the New Testament writers recognised most fully the inspiration of the Old Testament as leading to Christ, and were themselves inspired in declaring Christ and His doctrine. But, without making such assumptions as we have hitherto shunned, is it equally clear that as to every point of antecedent fact they were invested with infallibility? It is at least possible that while blest with a peculiar spiritual guidance, they were still left to avail themselves of the ordinary means in acquiring historical knowledge. The text of the New Testament, if closely examined, seems rather to indicate that they were guided, to some degree, not only by the Old Testament record, but by the current belief of the day. Indeed, it is doubtful how far those, who seem to press this argument to the fullest extent, would really trust themselves to it. It would be terrible indeed if we were obliged to propose either to ourselves or others such a dilemma as the following—either every reference of the New Testament writers to the old Jewish history is absolutely correct, or the New Testament does not contain an inspired revelation from God. Happily, it is much more clearly in our power to come to Christ than to fix a precise value on the texts which speak of Jannes and Jambres, or of the prophecy of Enoch, or of the contest of St Michael and Satan.

But an argument, the same in principle, but coming in a still more solemn form, in favour of the undoubted and absolute integrity of the old Jewish records, is built on the express reference made to them by our Lord. Portions of them appear thus to receive the most direct and authoritative sanction; and what is thus established of a part is then transferred to the whole. An argument such as this deserves our most serious and reverent

determined by the Substance of the Gospel. 109

consideration, even if it does not prove convincing. But it is clear that we cannot accept it as conclusive, unless we make the prior assumption, so easy to assume, but so difficult to prove, that the Evangelists always recorded, and the Gospels in their present state have always preserved, the very words of our Lord[1]. We know how slight a turn of a phrase may bar the retrospective force of an allusion, while it leaves its prospective reference untouched. And generally we may doubt how far it is safe or possible to hang upon a few detached passages, which our Lord has filled with the free spirit of the New Covenant, the entire letter of the Old. Indeed, do we know that it was part of His mission, who came to remove the law only by fulfilling it, to instruct the Church of that day on points of this nature, or to disturb at all, except by elevating it as a whole, the ordinary platform of existing knowledge? On holy ground like this it is perhaps well not to move a single step without the guidance of what is written. But when we read in the Gospel that Jesus in-

[1] Note XV.

creased in wisdom as well as in stature; that He spoke of a day and an hour of which the Son knew not, but the Father only; that He marvelled at the faith of the Centurion, and the unbelief of His countrymen[1],—we cannot doubt that our Lord, in assuming the body of our humiliation, condescended, in some real sense, to the veil of our ignorance[2]. Whatever be the real relation of the law and the Gospel, we know as a matter of history that it was not found at once. The schoolmaster was for a considerable time allowed to hold the infant Church by the hand, even after he had brought her to Christ, who is the true Teacher.

The general connection of the law and Gospel is undoubted. The Gospel is the substance, and the law the shadow—dark and mysterious, but real still. Would we trace its outline exactly, we must approach critically the ancient volume which contains its record. Wonderful indeed is the task which opens before us. The criticism of the New

[1] Luke ii. 52; Mark xiii. 32; Matth. xxiv. 36; Matth. viii. 10; Mark vi. 6; Luke vii. 9.
[2] Note XVI.

Testament is difficult, as those know who have made trial of it. What shall we say of the criticism of the Old Testament? Its historical compass is not embraced, like that of the New Testament, within the bounds of a century: it extends from the beginning of the world down to some four hundred years before the birth of Christ. Its events are not grouped around one distinct person, one bright and glorious centre; they derive their unity from a streak of light, sometimes marked and clear, but often all but interrupted, struggling backwards to that bright and glorious centre, from which it came, and in which it was again to terminate. We must begin our task, if we do not conclude it, in entire or comparative ignorance of the names, the dates, the authorities, of many of its writers. We can see in the record the marks of widely different times and circumstances, of varied and independent documents, of additions, omissions, revisions. The text has of course its variations even now; but it shows traces of still wider variations before one great and final recension, of whose merits we are probably poor judges. To bear upon it in its present state we must employ a great and complicated apparatus. The complete anatomy of a family of languages, in their formation, their growth, and their decay; the mysterious depths of ethnology, the history of early empires and buried dynasties, even the vast spaces and elementary forms of geology—all must be analysed that they may be arranged, and brought to bear upon the history of that strange people, at once so weak and so powerful; a marvel in their sins, their gifts, their destiny, whether beheld by the light of the Gospel, or without it.

It is, I trust, no wholly unfaithful feeling which makes some persons rejoice that, in the absence of an inward vocation, they have no outward vocation to a work like this. Happily it is no part of the duty of the ordinary Christian. From the sublime security of the Gospel we view the mysteries of the law. Guided by the example of Apostles and Evangelists, nay, of Christ Himself, we may be well content, when some special duty

determined by the Substance of the Gospel. 113

does not invite or compel us to another course, to let our minds dwell on those parts of the Old Testament of which we can perceive or feel the connection with the new covenant, abstaining from unnecessary scrutiny of the letter, when we cannot associate it with the living Spirit. But others may be called on to attempt a task to which we are not equal. Are they lovers of peace, and truth, and Christ? We may stand by watching them, sending our good wishes and our prayers after them in their perilous exploration, encouraging them with words of hope when their hands are weak and their hearts weary, protecting them as far as possible from the rude censure of those who raise their voices instinctively to swell any common cry, and are much more ready to condemn than to understand[1]. Let us see that we inherit the promises through patience as well as faith. Whether as enquirers or as simple observers, let us be more willing to wait than to dispute. Our judgment, in this as in other respects, may well catch the tem-

[1] Note XVII.

per of our devotion. As in the course of our services we read the Psalms, we often find, following on some touching passage of sorrow or penitence, or mingling even with the voice of love, the burning words of indignation, and the cry for revenge upon enemies. Then, though our lips proceed, our thoughts pause. We repeat the words, in a strong historical and personal sympathy with the man after God's own heart, and yet we feel that such language, and such thoughts and feelings, are not those of the Gospel, or ours. We lay them before God in the congregation, and pray Him to put His meaning upon them. A meaning they have in His providential purpose, though that meaning may not be David's, or our own. To Him, the living God, all men live; not Abraham, and Isaac, and Jacob only, but Moses, and David, and the Prophets; nay, every good wish and work, every noble aspiration, every true though imperfect prayer. And so we accept the utterances of the Old Testament writers, often not knowing precisely their force or import, (how *can*

determined by the Substance of the Gospel. 115

we know it when we know not who wrote them, or when, or why?) but leaving them to God, and waiting for His interpretation. Thus, from the height of the Gospel, we look down upon the law, and, through the law, to the immensities beyond it. These vast and uncertain distances of space and time may dazzle and confuse us; but, if we are not faint-hearted, we shall not fear, for, as we gaze, we lean on the eternal Arm. Far below us move and preach those ministers, through whom the Old Jewish world believed. We cannot catch their voices distinctly; but they are ours. In Christ, all things are ours; life and death, things present and things to come; the unborn future, and the dead law, and the living Gospel; Paul, and Apollos, and Cephas, and not these alone; but Moses and David and Isaiah, and the authors of Joshua, and Judges, and Ruth, and other books; compilers, arrangers, transcribers; all are ours, and we are Christ's, and Christ is God's.

SERMON V.

CHRIST, THE CENTRE OF CHRISTIAN TRUTH.

Preached in Christ Church Cathedral, 16 Dec. 1860.

1 JOHN III. 24.

Hereby we know that he abideth in us, by the Spirit which he hath given us.

OUR reflections on the nature and purposes of Holy Scripture have, as they have proceeded, changed their form without any real change of their substance. We began by considering its Inspiration. An endeavour was made to show, that when the devout and humble Christian speaks of the Bible as inspired, his primary, though not therefore his only meaning is this—that through it the Holy Spirit of God speaks to his spirit. If it be asked of what that Holy Spirit speaks, the answer is ready, Of Christ. The sacred volume, from beginning to end, finds it fulfilment in Him who is both the author and finisher of our faith. Is a further question made, through whom the Holy Spirit speaks? The general purpose of our answer is clear, though its details are not so definite. By the lips and the pens of the sacred writers God has spoken in time past; but He has spoken at sundry times and in divers manners. We can perceive the unity of His plan much more easily than we can understand the diversity of His operations. And that which is most easy is also most important. Discussions as to the authorship of disputed books, the state of the text of Holy Scripture, the mental condition of its writers, and the like, are questions of quite the second order. Most Christians can never entertain them at all; and generation upon generation of Christians cannot decide them. On points of this kind, one age begins a discussion; and another finishes it, if indeed it finish it. Meanwhile, every faithful heart demands, within the limits of its own few years of trial, the answer to another question—To whom does the Holy Spirit speak through the Bible? It is because we know the answer to this question, that we read the Bible in the congregation and in the closet. Through Holy Scripture, the Holy Spirit speaks to us—to us, separately and collectively, to the individual and to the Church. And thus the Inspiration of Holy Scripture cannot be viewed practically apart from the work of the Spirit in the heart of the believer. That which Holy Scripture gives, we receive. Though not itself the light, or the source of light, yet round it as round a centre, dark and cold perhaps without the informing Spirit, is gathered much of the glory of Him, who lighteth every man that cometh into the world. The grace of the Holy Spirit does not depend upon it for existence; rather its own existence, as an illumining and life-giving power, depends entirely upon the grace of the Holy Spirit. Its virtue we know by what it is allowed to do for us. We derive our conception of its inherent light and warmth from the light and warmth which it diffuses in the spiritual atmosphere around us. Its beams, direct and reflected, give us the guidance which suffices for our daily walk. That guidance is not the less real, though we cannot exactly test the brilliancy of the orb from which it comes. We recognise it in our system as the centre of a divine illumination, an illumination, however, which would dazzle and not direct us, were not its glories diffused and tempered by the Divine hand that made them, till they fade into the light of common day, which is God's light still.

If this be so, it is no wonder that the phraseology of the schools, which is only exceptionally and partially used in Holy Scripture, and is never employed in our own authorised formularies[1], is far from being the only means of expressing important truths, which we need for our everyday guidance. Among those who feel most reluctant and unequal to discuss the Inspiration of the Bible, are perhaps to be found those who are most near to understanding it. It is always dangerous,

[1] Note XVIII.

in practical matters, habitually to express a concrete truth in an abstract form. Our words then run the risk of being emptied of their best meaning, in becoming dissevered if not from our thoughts, at least from our feelings and actions. It is good, were it only by way of precaution, to recall them from time to time from the height of abstraction, and to test their weight at the level on which we have to use them. We believe that Holy Scripture is inspired, when we believe that God's Holy Spirit has caused it to be written for our instruction in the things of Christ. We believe in its full or plenary inspiration, not in accepting, prior to sufficient enquiry, this or that theory about its structure, or criticism, or contents, but in believing that it is all intended to teach us a Divine lesson, whatever that lesson may be. We believe in the Inspiration of its writers in recognising the important truth, that the same Holy Spirit, which teaches us who read, taught them who wrote. Other men have laboured, and we have entered into their labours.

Of the nature of this Divine lesson we

should speak, it would seem, at once confidently and diffidently—confidently, in virtue of our Divine teacher, but diffidently, because we are learners still. Its substance we know from one of the ablest and most blessed of its teachers—" Christ crucified—the Power of God and the Wisdom of God[1];" perfect love and purity working, suffering, dying, rising, triumphing in the form of man, that man also may be changed into the same image from glory to glory, even as by the Spirit of the Lord. In Him "neither circumcision availeth anything, nor uncircumcision, but a new creature." "As many as walk according to this rule, peace be on them, and mercy, and upon the Israel of God[2]."

And here the many pause; or, rather, it were good if they proceeded so far. The work of Christ for us, and the work of Christ in us, are surely the great lessons of the Gospel and its attendant system. We are not unapt pupils in His school, if we have really learned that it is our duty to be like Him, our privilege to approach God in and through

[1] 1 Cor. i. 23, 24. [2] Gal. vi. 15, 16.

Him. His word leads us from darkness to light, from slavery to the freedom of the Kingdom, from man to God, from time to eternity. This is the order in which He trains our hearts, and, for the most part, trains our minds also. Yet there are times in the history, both of the Church, and of many individual minds, at which the intellectual order seems reversed. Some great change in our mental or moral condition, some shock, it may be, to preconceived belief, or some sudden accession to our knowledge, disturbs for the time, what it cannot destroy, the harmony between the outer and inner world. New fields of enquiry may be opening, new ideas becoming prominent; fresh dry land may be rising above the sea, peopled with strange forms of life. Arts and sciences, hitherto unknown or uncultivated, may be flocking together, each bearing its offering to the great temple of truth, but each speaking as yet in its own peculiar and unusual language, and, even if their hearts and thoughts are one, not knowing how to raise their voices in harmony. Vast gulfs here open on the thoughtful mind. The horizon of time widens, and in widening threatens to dissolve; and eternity seems to tremble with it. Our frail humanity feels its weakness in the reaction from some new victory which its powers have won. The eye looks forth upon so many marvels that it almost distrusts its own power of seeing. The active world pauses for a moment in the midst of its action to wonder. Of the comparatively few who can really think, some doubt, a few enquire, fewer still analyse. As a condition of evolving a nobler future from the present, these few examine what the present involves. Thread by thread they scrutinise the complex cord which the Divine Providence has twisted. From action, they turn to history; from the ordinary processes of inference, they betake themselves to those great mysteries which underlie the human mind itself; accepting, as from God, the Divine message which they receive through human messengers, they enquire in what sense, and under what limitations, the Divine message is human. There is nothing wrong in such enquiries, though there are many dangers. They should not be undertaken rashly; but they should not be decried rashly. In the fulness of God's purpose, many dark, and bending, and interrupted lines meet in the centre of His love. It is the privilege of all true Christians to walk in the light which streams from that centre; it is the duty of some to examine the lines which lead to it, to count, if they can, their interruptions, and measure their deflections, and watch the last ray of light as it fades into darkness. Those who undertake such a work may exercise a high act of faith in so doing; those who do not and should not undertake it will render a simple obedience to the command of their Divine Master in abstaining from judging those who do. To whichever class we belong, one duty is clearly incumbent on us all—that of seeking, and speaking, and holding the Truth, or that which we believe to be the Truth, in love. Cool, accurate, polished intellect, going straight to its mark in the calm confidence of power, without any regard to the peace it may disturb, the faith it may unsettle, the consciences it may wound, has no promise from God. The conflict of opinion may be as selfish as that of war; and the selfish combatant has no right to expect a blessing. Nor can we expect any direct good from the labours of those, whose argument is sharpened with bitterness, and who carry the inflamed passions of earth to their scrutiny of the things of heaven.

On the other hand, a heavy responsibility certainly rests with those who deny their Christian sympathy to the honest seeker after Christian truth, and allow minds, isolated by their originality as well as their earnestness and power, to become isolated in feeling also. It is sad to run any risk of turning an eager champion of the truth into an intellectual gladiator, striking at his brethren with a sword which he had dedicated to a better purpose, the foe of others, and his own. A solemn woe is denounced against those through whom offences come. Before we apply this woe to others, we should be quite sure who are the real offenders. The guilt of offence often lies at the door of those who assume the position of injured defenders, and seek or make an occasion of offence, where the children of peace do not find one.

As to the results of the legitimate criticism of Holy Scripture, those perhaps will prophesy with the greatest confidence, who have least knowledge of the subject. It is certainly no duty of Christians in general to anticipate them, or to be anxious about them. In spiritual as in temporal things, it is well to be content with our daily bread, and to take no thought for the morrow, while we do the work of to-day. The results, be they what they may, have no direct or immediate bearing on our present subject—the Inspiration of Holy Scripture. If the lesson conveyed should prove to be not exactly what we have hitherto thought, still the Teacher is Divine, and we are the learners. In this faith we can safely trust to the Divine providence the interpretation of the Book which the Divine Wisdom has written. Nor must we be surprised if the clouds of our ignorance shift before they disperse, or seem to expand in the very act of dispersing. Our danger lies not in waiting, but in rashness—in rash attempts to recast the whole body of truth, in equally rash attempts to petrify all its existent forms, and identify those forms with the substance. He was not the greatest or the boldest of men, but not one of the worst or most unwise, who, on a certain memorable occasion, when a few busy men seemed to be shaking the foundations of an old and venerable system, gave in a solemn assembly the following advice:—"Refrain from these men, and let them alone: for if this counsel or work be of men, it will come to nought: but if it be of God, ye cannot overthrow it; lest haply ye be found even to fight against God[1]." The Pharisees agreed to him; and seem to have thought that they acted in the spirit of his advice by calling the Apostles, and beating them before they let them go. But *they* ceased not to teach and preach Jesus Christ, till an ally arose from a quarter whence they little expected it. A few short years of persecution, and dispersion, and struggle; and

[1] Acts v. 38, 39.

the Spirit of Paul leapt forth from the school of Gamaliel.

But if it is foreign to the duty of a Christian to spend his time and his thoughts in vain anticipations of the possible future, it is part of his duty to have regard to the living and actual present. And if he should carefully watch the whole course of Providence, that he may stand where God has placed him, and do the work which God has set before him, he certainly should not be regardless of those means of providential teaching, which are placed before him in the Church. For his practical purposes, of course, the Church will be primarily the Church of his own place and time. He should not restrict his sympathies to it; these should be broad as the whole congregation of Christian men dispersed throughout the world. If he is a thinker and a student, his thoughts and his researches will take a much wider range than his own day, and country, and communion. Still, if he accept the guidance of God's providence, he should surely, in this as in other matters, try not to place himself in some ideal position, but to work upon the very facts with which he finds himself in contact. Other leaders we can choose if we will, and serve them: but our natural allegiance is to the present Church; and, except by an act of self-will, conscious or unconscious, that natural allegiance cannot be transferred to the Church of the future or the Church of the past. We have no right to attempt an escape from any difficulties attendant on our position, by hurrying forward to indefinite possibilities, or by turning backward to a life and history, which, however definite, are not ours. But the student need scarcely be reminded that the air of definiteness, which, in the retrospect, belongs to the Church of any period when thought has been active and life energetic, is only a delusion caused by distance. Men of the fourth and fifth centuries were much like men of the present day. On disputed questions good men often did not know which side to take. Motives of policy and considerations of state were mingled with the love of truth: a few great men were doing battle at the call of a strong inner impulse; the multitude was raising its voice, now on this side, now on that; quiet and prayerful spirits were longing for the wings of a dove. We must be content in our day to labour like those who have gone before us, and to wait for the eternal peace. We cannot give to the Church a personality which is not hers, that she may speak with the distinct articulation of a single man, and the authority almost of God. It is possible, no doubt, by a certain exercise of imagination, to place her on a lofty throne, and hail her as a queen and a mother. To her, as also to the Virgin Mother of Christ, may be addressed the language of poetical apostrophe, till it sounds like that of prayer. But the metaphor, in either case, too often terminates in a sad reality. The handmaid of the Lord is placed upon the throne of her Son; and the bride of Christ closes the Bible.

The error, of course, lies not in the metaphor, but in its misapplication. The reader of the Gospel can still almost see Christ looking round, and stretching His hand towards His disciples, and saying, "Behold my mother and my brethren! for whosoever shall do the will of my Father which is in heaven, the same is my brother, and sister, and mother." Few thoughts are more exalting and cheering than that of the spiritual company—Christ the head, the many members the body, the bond which unites them the Holy Ghost, the Lord and giver of life, who spake by the prophets. Silently and quietly, like that of old, the new temple rises, "a spiritual house, a holy priesthood, to offer up spiritual sacrifices, acceptable to God by Jesus Christ." "Ye are a chosen generation, a royal priesthood, a holy nation, a peculiar people; that ye should shew forth the praises of Him who hath called you out of darkness into His marvellous light; which in time past were not a people, but are now the people of God; which had not obtained mercy, but now have obtained mercy[1]." Of them it is written in the Prophets, they shall be all taught of God. His word is in their hands, and His law in their hearts. Hereafter, a great multitude which no man can number, of all nations, and

[1] 1 Pet. ii. 5, 9, 10.

kindreds, and people, and tongues, they shall stand before the throne. Even now, their conversation is in heaven, from whence also they look for the Saviour, the Lord Jesus Christ.

On some such picture as this the heart reposes in faith, and not without the best of warrants. Yet how obscurely it answers to the facts. How great is the tossing and troubling of the Ark of Christ. On what a restless ocean do we look forth from its windows. Those who are by profession strangers and pilgrims to a heavenly kingdom do not abstain from fleshly lusts which war against the soul. Their conversation is not honest among the Gentiles, but a disgrace and rebuke to the Gospel. Those who lead a better life are still divided in heart and opinion. Churches and individuals cry, "I am of Paul, and I of Apollos, and I of Cephas;" till they seem to forget that they are all of Christ. The House is divided against itself, till its foes predict that it will soon fall, and its friends often wonder that it stands.

Yet among all this diversity, we believe

that there is a root of unity. The unity is of God, the diversity of man. The spiritual temple is built on Christ as its foundation, though the walls be rent asunder, from the battlements to the very ground. Since divisions began (and how soon did they not begin?) the wish and the prayer of all good men has been for unity. The prayer cannot have been ineffectual, though its results have not been visible. Perhaps, in the spirit of Him who broke down the middle wall of partition, good men, hidden from each other by the divisions of Christendom, have been walking much nearer to each other in Christ than has appeared to themselves and the world. In this way, those who are separated by time and place and language and opinion and communion may be close to each other now. "Neither death, nor life, nor angels, nor principalities, nor powers, nor things present, nor things to come, nor height, nor depth, nor any other creature, shall be able to separate us from the love of God, which is in Christ Jesus our Lord[1]." Would we have a visible symbol of

[1] Rom. viii. 38, 39.

our common privilege? Do we seek, in no unfaithful spirit, an outward sign of this inward and spiritual grace? By building on one foundation alone can we hope to repair the breaches of our Zion. Without disregarding a single indication of that providence which surrounds us, without cutting a single tie which binds us to our brethren, nay, drawing tighter the cords of love in the strength of a living faith, we must go, as pilgrims though not as strangers, through all the centuries to the first—past reformer, and schoolman, and father, nay, past Apostles and Evangelists themselves, to the Sermon on the Mount and the Hill of Calvary.

The present is not an occasion on which to discuss the value and nature of church formularies. Suffice it to say, that whatever be their use, they must rank as authorities far below the Bible. Could we collect, compile, compare, the whole doctrinal formularies of the existing universal Church, correct their language till they expressed accurately the present state of feeling and opinion, modify or explain if we could not remove their differences, and expand their points of general agreement, we should then construct a document which would stand historically in somewhat the same relation to the existing Church, in which the New Testament stands to the days of the first and fullest outpouring of the Spirit. It would contain, we trust, all essential truth, as expressing, among many contradictions of the letter, the spirit of the body which Christ has promised to guide. But happily, essential truth is attainable in a much simpler form. The sacred work of those early days, ready in all our hands, saves us from any necessity of attempting an impossible work now. But if the formularies of the Universal Church are inaccessible in any available shape, those of particular Churches are of necessity partial and imperfect. Were we to dwell on their diversities, their letter would indeed kill; but their spirit helps to save, so far as it is the Spirit of Christ. We can exempt no formulary from this subordination to the written Word. The most venerable creeds cannot rise above the Scriptures from which they are drawn. Their virtue lies in those Gospel truths which were in the Church from the first. If they contain additions of a later philosophy, or are at all tinged by the passions or opinions of particular times and persons, it is not from these peculiarities that they derive their power. Old truths may filter through the minds of generations, and rise again in some new form at Nicæa, at Constantinople, or some now unknown place in France or Spain; but their highest level is fixed by that of the living water which once fell from heaven upon the now barren mountains of Judæa. The concise and exact character of the creeds, so far as it is an advantage, must not be taken to result from any addition of matter, but from a diminution of scale. The outline is hard, because it is reduced; it must be magnified once more, before we can discern and employ its details. The Gospel narratives of the Passion are none the less necessary because the Apostles' Creed declares that Christ suffered under Pontius Pilate. The most formal statement of our Lord's humanity has less intrinsic preciousness than two short words of Scripture—'Jesus wept.' The fulness of creeds is from Holy Scripture, as that of Holy Scripture is from Christ.

From Him, the one Head, proceeds the Holy Spirit to and through His members. In Him alone, we believe, meet, in absolute perfection, the Divine and the Human. To His Spirit we ascribe the relative perfection of Holy Scripture. We accept it humbly and gratefully, confident that it is perfectly fitted for its sacred work, but not equally confident in detail what the nature of that work may be. The same Holy Spirit which gives it its life and power, stirs also in the solitary believing heart, and in the corporate heart of the Church. The Church, no longer a little band, fades insensibly into the world: and there also the Spirit has its witness; for there we find many things true, honest, pure, lovely, and of good report; and all these things are of God.

The scattered and diffused light is good; the concentred light is better; the source of light itself is better still. The work of the world is lower than the work of the Church; the Church fulfils its function, in impressing on those within and those without its pale the great truths of the Bible; these truths have then only their free course, when they lead men to Christ. The means are best appreciated when they are seen to be means, not ends. Perhaps we are seldom nearer to Christ, than when, though the Bible be for the time closed, its lesson is still fresh in our hearts, and we kneel humbly before the mercy seat, thinking of nothing but our sinfulness and our Saviour. Perhaps the Churches would lose no real privilege, if, resolving as much as possible their separate teaching into that of Holy Scripture, and seeing nothing so clearly in Holy Scripture as the life and work of Christ, they repented of much premature assertion and much needless isolation, and clung as weeping Magdalenes to the foot of the Cross. To that Cross it is to be hoped that we can all come without an exact knowledge of the means which lead us thither. Would we enquire further of those means? Let us be careful, while we do so, still to walk guardedly in the narrow way, as disciples of Him who is the Way, the Truth, and the Life; to exclude moral sins from the process of intellectual enquiry, and to strive, not only to be faithful and reverent, but to be just, and tolerant, and kind.

SERMON VI.

THE METHOD OF LOVE.

Preached at St Mary's Church, 9 June, 1861.

1 CORINTHIANS VIII. 1—3.

Knowledge puffeth up, but charity edifieth. And if any man think that he knoweth any thing, he knoweth nothing yet as he ought to know. But if any man love God, the same is known of him.

IN a series of Sermons addressed to this University, I have endeavoured to lay before my hearers, in a manner which was meant to be connected, some considerations on the Inspiration of Holy Scripture. I have spoken of it as of an organised whole, a letter, dead by itself, but living, because associated with a living Spirit, and that Spirit, the Spirit of Christ. And as in living and organised beings

The Method of Love. 141

there are many members and diversities of functions, each useful in its place, but not all equally important, some simply for use, some also decked with ornament, some necessary for life, some for sense, some for ease and enjoyment, so we may expect to find in Holy Scripture great varieties of structure, of necessity, and use. Nay, we are all agreed that we *do* find them. All Scripture is profitable, but not all Scripture equally profitable. Were we, with unstored memories, allowed only, during an illness or imprisonment, the use of a certain number of pages taken from the Bible, we should be right in choosing for the companions of our solitude the four Gospels rather than the two books of Chronicles. In translating the Bible for the use of the heathen, no sensible translator would think it a matter of indifference, which part of the sacred volume he first prepared for their hands. There is an order and arrangement of less and greater even in things Divine. The Son Himself said, " the Father is greater than I." Nay, things Divine, equal in one sense, may still be unequal in another ;

as we repeat of the Son—"equal to the Father as touching His Godhead; and inferior to the Father as touching His Manhood." Thus there is no impropriety in saying of the Sacred Volume, that it is all sacred, yet not all equally sacred. The consecrating Spirit is in it everywhere, and yet not everywhere in the same way. No one here present, I suppose, doubts that the proportion of Spirit to letter, of outward visible sign to inward spiritual grace, of type and thing typified, of ceremonial law and spiritual freedom, is different under the Christian and under the Jewish Dispensation. And the difference which exists between the Dispensations is morally sure to leave its traces in the Record. The most faithful portraits of the same person would not be identical, if, in one case, the person portrayed wore a veil, in the other not. There is no veil now; that is done away in Christ; but still there is not perfect illumination. We still see through a glass darkly. We see imperfectly, partly from the necessary limitation of our finite nature; partly, from the imperfect light which it has pleased God as yet to cast upon many of His works and words; partly, from the dim and sickly mist which is spread over the mirror of our consciousness by our sins. And of this our imperfect knowledge — an imperfect knowledge of God's written word, as of other things—an imperfect knowledge of its writers, of the nature and degree of their spiritual illumination, of the exact text which they wrote, of their exact meaning in writing it, of the interpretation which they themselves would have put upon their own writings, of the interpretation which the Divine Providence, in its ceaseless onward course, is ever giving to the Divine Word, as the old text receives a new comment, and the present, gathering up the stores of the past, looks on to the unfolding future—of this imperfect knowledge we need an order and arrangement. Such an arrangement, in matters of ordinary knowledge, we call a Science: such an arrangement, in things of God and the Soul, we call Theology. And one condition of a legitimate arrangement in either case, is that it should be at once fixed, and expansive—fixed at its centre, expansive at its circumference; clinging to old truths, and yet receptive of new; never letting a fact drop, which it has once apprehended, and never repelling from its system any proved, established fact, to seek another home. Such should our science be, and such our theology; firm and yet fluctuating; penetrated by a real stirring life; with a changing, because a growing outline; not ignoring fresh accessions of truth, but accepting and arranging them; open as the truth which it seeks, and all-embracing as charity.

The centre of our theology, happily, none of us have to seek. When men would attain to the knowledge of God, a voice from the Divine Book answers—" He that hath seen Me hath seen the Father[1]." Nowhere but to Christ do we look for the perfect harmony of the Godhead and Manhood. His Life is the Idea from which all the precious facts of Christianity derive their unity; His goodness is the perfect type of which the imperfect goodness of His servants is the imperfect

[1] John xiv. 9.

The Method of Love. 145

image and copy. To Him bear all the prophets witness; the antecedents of His coming are chronicled by Old Testament historians, and by heathen writers also; Evangelists tell of His Life and Death; Apostles record and propagate His doctrine. From Him proceeds the pure light of truth; round Him, as He sits on His throne, is seen a rainbow as an emerald—an iris of many coloured hues, truly light, yet not unmixed light. Do our eyes fail to catch, or our words to express, each delicate shade of colour? Do we try in vain to draw imaginary lines, which shall complete our analysis and arrangement, separate tint from tint, divide light from darkness, and entitle us to say, Here is the pure ray of Divine Truth; and there, starless as well as sunless, the night of human error? Are we glorying too soon in having found a faultless arrangement of Divine truth, or despairing too soon because after anxious and honest search we cannot find one? Let us listen to a few words of one who was in darkness while he thought he saw, and whom the first accession of real light dazzled even to blindness—"Knowledge puffeth up, but charity edifieth. And if any man think that he knoweth anything, he knoweth nothing yet as he ought to know. But if any man love God, the same is known of Him."

"Knowledge puffeth up, but charity edifieth." We lose in this translation a portion of the antithetical force which belongs to the original. We may either follow the Vulgate—"Scientia inflat, charitas vero ædificat,"—"Knowledge inflates, but charity edifies;" or adopting a phraseology more purely English, may say, "Knowledge puffs up, but love builds up." There is real expansion in knowledge, but it is an expansion of self. It may be fair and shapely, beautiful in form and colour, and float proudly along, reflecting earth and heaven; but still it is a bubble full of our own perishing breath; often thinnest when greatest, tossed to and fro by the winds of the merest fancy, and pierced to its destruction by a single inconvenient fact. But grant it as true and genuine and lasting as mere knowledge can be, this does not rid it of its one fatal limitation; it comes from self, and, of itself, can go no further. After all, my knowledge is only what *I* have felt, *I* have thought, *I* have argued. My own consciousness is the fact; my existence, or that of my brother, or that of my Maker, only the inference. In increasing our knowledge, we increase our sorrow, because we increase our loneliness. We think that we have gained a common heritage of truth; but we look more closely at it, and find it branded with the ineffaceable mark of our own wretched individuality. We collect facts, trace consequences, draw inductions, perceive and connect resemblances; we tell things by their number and weight, register their order and uniformity, and think that we have found a law—something independent of ourselves on which we can rely, and know (as if that were worth the knowing) that it remains, though we perish. But then psychology steps in, all imperfect itself, yet potent enough to spoil our imperfect physics. How can the mind, it asks, know anything beyond itself? Mould and shape your consciousness how you please, it is *your* consciousness still. Matter, be it what it may, is to you only what *you* see, *you* feel, *you* handle; and your sight, your touch, all your powers of mind and body, are yours, and yours alone. How can you pass beyond yourself, when your own senses are your chains, and your faculties are the bars of your prison? You sit in the twilight, you know not whether of evening or of morning, and see a form before you. You move, and it moves; you speak to it, and think you have found a friend. But it is your own shadow that you address; it may be altered and distorted, but still your shadow, cast forward on the fluctuating mist by the unseen sun behind you. You cry aloud in the despair of your solitude, and voices seem to answer: but they are only the echoes of your own voice, tossed to and fro in airy mockery among the misty heads of the mountains. And so knowledge runs its course, all confidence and inflation at first; then, all despair and isolation; at last, perhaps, all coldness and indifference. "The thing that hath been, it is that which shall be; and that which is done, is that which shall be done;

and there is no new thing under the sun. Vanity of vanities, saith the Preacher, all is vanity[1]."

But, happily, we have spoken only of a portion of our text, and that the negative portion. If knowledge isolates, love unites; if knowledge inflates, charity edifies; if knowledge puffs up, love builds up; if knowledge expands self, love annihilates self:

> Love was given,
> Encouraged, sanctioned, chiefly for that end;
> That self might be annulled: her bondage prove
> The fetters of a dream, opposed to love[2].

Love builds up the loving heart on a foundation, and that foundation is a Person. Conceptions, facts, phenomena, laws, suffice her not. She sees them, but rests not on them. They are to her not ultimate truths, but the outward garb and vestments of truth. They have no soul or spirit: and she claims a Spirit to answer to her spirit. Kneeling, she touches just the fringes of the garment, the texture of which knowledge is scrutinising; but He who wears it, He who is clothed with honour and

[1] Ecclesiastes i.   [2] Wordsworth.

majesty, and covers Himself with light as with a garment, looks on her in mercy, and strengthens her conscious weakness. And thus love edifies herself and others, by going out of herself. By the exercise of a prophetic and instinctive power she feels after God and finds Him, perceiving the Maker in His works, the Lawgiver behind the law. And our love of our fellow-creatures is in this respect like our love of our Creator. It is through affection and feeling, not through reason, that man recognises his fellow-man. Morbid thought at times may almost persuade him that he is alone in the world, with no being like himself; but one strong and lively emotion, one current of sympathy from another toward ourselves, or from ourselves toward another, is enough to break through the web of abstractions which our own reflectiveness has spun around us. But we need not now insist on any points of resemblance or difference between man's love to God and his love to his fellow-man. The Gospel unites, combines, almost identifies them. "This commandment have we from Him, that he who loveth God love his brother also[1]." And so in the context of the passage which we are now considering, "through thy knowledge shall the weak brother perish, for whom Christ died?" "When ye sin so against the brethren, and wound their weak conscience, ye sin against Christ." Love to our brother in Christ is love to man in Him who is both God and man. To Him it is our privilege to turn, when the complex cord of our knowledge seems untwisting, and losing its strength by separation, as to One who loved us before we loved Him, One who knows all who love Him, One who completes the weakness of our knowledge by the strength of His love, and gives to our life a worthy aim, and to our whole being a unity.

And thus, my brethren, we are led to one important question, which closely concerns us all. We have, I trust, often in our hands, and very near to our hearts, a wonderful volume, the volume of God's written word. It tells us, like other ancient books, what once passed through the minds of men now long gone to their rest; but, unlike other ancient

[1] 1 John iv. 21.

books, it stands in a declared and traceable relation to the eternal purposes of an ever-living Spirit. By that Holy Spirit it is inspired; and His work of inspiration terminates not in itself. He, Himself a person and a spirit, would guide our personal spirits onward and upward to another Person, the object of Christian faith, the channel of Christian worship, even the Son of God, in whom we see, and through whom we have access to, the Father.

How shall we treat this book—this precious instrument and token of a more precious personality behind it? Shall we adopt with regard to it the order of knowledge, or that of love? Shall we think that the most elaborate apparatus of our own conceptions has any real power in matters of religion either to construct or to destroy? Shall we try to define the inspiration of that Spirit of whom it is said in a figure, that He bloweth where He listeth, and we hear the sound thereof, but cannot tell whence He cometh or whither He goeth? Shall we assume some human formula of our own or another's making; arrange by its aid, according to the rules of art, the words of Holy Writ; deduce our conclusions therefrom with logical severity, and embrace the results as theological truths, worth the seeking, or worth the having? Alas, this method has been tried in the easiest and most humble departments of truth, and been found wanting. This scholastic procedure has proved itself unable to carry the human intellect to a point from which it can take a just and truthful view of the things of earth; much less can it teach the human soul to soar on the wings of its own abstractions to the very vaults of heaven. We know what has been the fate of ordinary mediæval science, conducted as it often was in all good faith and in full sincerity of purpose, but building unconsciously on self instead of seeking a foundation out of self; saying innocently yet proudly (so far as pride can be innocent), "I know," when it knew nothing yet as it ought to know. The builders, we trust, are saved, though their work has perished, and left men wondering how it stood even for a time, built as it was on the fluctuating sands of opinion, and quite at the mercy of those simple yet stubborn facts, which, instead of incorporating, it ignored.

But some one may say or think—and such words and such thoughts are more native to this place than to most others—"No doubt, science was presumptuous of old, and is presumptuous now. It does not know its place or its province, but thrusts its crude guesses and unproved assertions into the province of that queenly science, Theology. It is this false knowledge which puffs up, misleads, subverts—premature geology, imperfect history, vain metaphysical speculation, rising up in opposition to the firm and solid truth." Nay, my brother, can we or should we except theology from the scope of the Apostle's words—"Knowledge puffs up, but charity edifies: and if any man think that he knoweth any thing, he knoweth nothing yet as he ought to know"? Is not the very subject of which the Apostle is speaking the great elementary truth of Christian theology?—"An idol is nothing in the world, and there is none other God but one. To us there

The Method of Love. 155

is but one God, the Father, of whom are all things, and we in Him; and one Lord Jesus Christ, by whom are all things, and we by Him." Does theology (I mean of course a theology which is pursued on a faulty method, and cultivated in an imperfect temper) never puff up, inflate, undo the work of charity? Are physical and historical science so wholly wrong, if they present as their contribution to truth the results of observation and reflection, confessing at the same time that these results are only hypotheses, and that they know nothing yet as they ought to know? Will Theology forfeit her lawful position by accepting in humility what they offer in honesty, and, like a wise householder, bringing forth out of her treasures things old and new? Will she be less truly royal, if she does not exercise over other sciences a lordship like that of the kings of the Gentiles, but rather, like her own Divine Lord, is, though the greatest, among them as the youngest, a servant, though really the chief? Surely she has a noble work before her; for she is a ruler still, but no despot. She can arbitrate where she cannot dominate, can poise the balance of opinion, relieve the pressure of doubt, break the violence of controversy, trace amid apparent discords the finer harmonies of science, and point in hope toward the final adjustment of truths which she cannot contradict.

But, among all the difficulties which beset the harmony of our many-sided and imperfect knowledge, shall not we, my brethren, as we read the Bible, employ the simple yet effectual method of love? It is true as a general rule (the few sad exceptions to which few of us can be called on to analyse) that learned and unlearned alike derive from the study of the Gospels, as Apostles derived from the presence of Christ in the flesh, a sense that the holiness of His Manhood involves more than manhood, and that the worship, which we owe to God alone, is His right, and our privilege. And thus a finite spirit learns to converse with an Infinite Spirit in Love. Prayer, praise, repentance, a holy life, love toward our fellow-men, all are parts of the language in which we learn to speak to Him. His Church, His Sacraments, His Providence, His Written Word, the love of His children to one another, all are symbols through which He, using the language of our imperfect faculties, expresses, so far as we can yet receive it, His love and His will to us. His Spirit speaks to our spirit, as we read the sacred page, which tells of Him, His precursors and followers. Its inspiration is a fact to us, far above all theories. We wish to listen, not to define; to open every portal of our soul, and catch every holy utterance; not to determine beforehand what the Holy Spirit must or shall say, but to reply in our hearts to the Divine voice, "Speak, Lord, for thy servant heareth."

That we *may* hear, we must listen in love. If we are without love, the very faculty which receives Divine Truth is wanting. "He that loveth not," the beloved disciple tells us, "knoweth not God; for God is Love[1]." Theology, if a loveless knowledge, is a mere trick of words and a playing with notions, like the talk of a blind man about

[1] 1 John iv. 8.

colours. But love can never be really ignorant. She has that within herself which knowledge labours to express, and cannot. Her primary fact is that without which the heart is dead, the eye of the soul dark, all knowledge vain, all inference a mockery—the Love which descends from God to man, and ascends from man to God.

Happily, we have often more love than appears on the surface; or the controversies of the Christian world would be a sadder spectacle even than they are. Old sins hang about us, and spoil our powers of expression, as fathers of old, when they became Christians, never quite ceased to be Greek rhetoricians. The very warmth of love, in an imperfect temper, may simulate the heat of anger, and our words and manner catch an unfelt bitterness. Moral indignation is sometimes by mistake cultivated as if it were a virtue, and not rather an expression of virtuous feeling, which is right only when it is unforced and natural. And some natures there are, of no low type, but somewhat disproportioned, whose large heart is fettered by a narrow mind, and whose undue heat often marks the point at which their power of reasoning or understanding ceases, just as the galvanic wire grows hot where it is finest and therefore weakest. But, when all due allowance is made, the sad fact remains—our speculations about Holy Scripture are marked by too little love. Were love more abundantly present, we should be much less ready to assert hastily what would pain our brother, or to meet hasty assertion with equally hasty contradiction. We should treat with much more tenderness every form of religious thought which experience shews us to be compatible with devotion and goodness. We should look with a deeper sympathy on the creeds, and forms, and worship of all the churches; knowing that Christ is in the midst of any two or three who are gathered together in His name, and that words which are quite imperfect as statements of speculative truth, may yet, when they fall from pure and clean lips, be genuine outpourings of love to Him. Difficult questions, which simple folk cannot entertain, and which the learned entertain but cannot agree in answering, we should feel to be quite subordinate to the duty of Christian charity. The eye of love, if it wandered from time to time over the whole field of Christian truth, would find its way back habitually to Christ the centre, and rest there. Knowledge might scrutinise anxiously the forms that move in the distant and imperfect twilight; but love would find her home and her happiness in turning to the Light itself.

Does any one read his Bible with a real love to Christ and his brethren, and a deep sense of his own unworthiness and ignorance? Does he say from his heart, "I would embrace all truth, and deny none; I have no faith in the riddles of psychology; I am perplexed with evidence and counter-evidence, and have no clue of my own with which to combine the broken and scattered facts of history: but I learn from the Bible to love Christ, and put my trust in Him; and He alone is my Master"? If such there be, whether he speak in love, or in love hold silence, let him not trouble himself curiously in this

The Method of Love.

matter, and let not others trouble him. He bears in his soul, if not in his body, the marks of the Lord Jesus. "For in Christ Jesus neither circumcision availeth anything, nor uncircumcision; but a new creature. And as many as walk according to this rule, peace be on them, and mercy, and upon the Israel of God[1]."

[1] Galatians *ad fin*.

NOTES.

SERMON I.

NOTE I. p. 4.

In all probability, the proper rendering of the text is, "Every Scripture, being inspired by God, is also profitable, &c." If so, St Paul still pronounces the whole of the Old Testament Scriptures to be inspired. The epithet loses none of its force by being shifted from the predicate to the subject. It is true that many versions omit καὶ in v. 16; but this negative evidence cannot stand against the positive authority of the MSS. There is no real ground for supposing that St Paul meant to say "every writing, so far as it is inspired by God, is profitable," &c.

NOTE II. p. 7.

The conversion of St Paul cannot well be placed later than seven years from the ascension. I am not aware that any competent critic claims so early a date for the Gospels. The most received opinion seems to be, that St Matthew's Gospel is the earliest, and that this was not written till thirty years after the ascension. Be this as it may, it is to the last degree unlikely that St Paul, at the time of his conversion, had access to any of our written Gospels. It cannot indeed be *proved* that he ever saw a written Gospel.

NOTE III. p. 10.

Individuals, it is universally allowed, did not precisely agree about the Canon in the fourth and fifth centuries. The case is much the same with Councils. The Canon, as we accept it, was practically formed in the latter part of the fourth century. But the Council of Laodicea (circ. A.D. 365) does not include the Revelation in its list, if indeed, that list be genuine; while the third Council of Carthage, which met some thirty years later, completes indeed the Canon of the New Testament as we receive it, but also reckons the Wisdom of Solomon, Tobit, Judith, and two Books of Maccabees, as Canonical Scriptures. These were of course provincial Councils; the Church universal of that day made no decree on the subject.

Mr Westcott, in his able and learned work on the *Canon of the New Testament*, calls attention in the following passage to the remarkable fact, that the Church of England has not defined beyond reach of dispute the Canon of the Sacred Volume.

"The authoritative teaching of the Church of England on the Canon of the New Testament is not removed beyond all question. In the Articles of 1552 it was affirmed that 'Holy Scripture containeth all things necessary to salvation,' but nothing was then said of the books included under that title. In the Elizabethan Articles of 1562 (and 1571) a definition was added: 'in the name of Holy Scripture we do understand those Canonical books of the Old and New Testament of whose authority was never any doubt in the Church.' Then follows a statement 'Of the names and number of the Canonical books,' in which the books of the Old Testament are enumerated at length. A list of the Old Testament Apocrypha is given next, imperfect in the Latin, but complete in the English; and at the end it is said: 'all the books of the New Testament, as they are commonly received, we do receive and account them for Canonical;' but no list is given. A strict interpretation of the language of the article thus leaves a difference between 'canonical books' and 'such canonical books as have never been doubted in the Church.'"

Mr Westcott is inclined to think it possible that "the framers of our Articles were willing to allow a certain freedom of opinion on a question which was left undecided, not only by the Lutheran, but by many Calvinistic Churches." He adds, however:—"I am not aware that the judgment of the English Church, as expressed by her theologians, has ever varied as to the canonical authority of any of the books of the New Testament. If she left her sons at liberty to test the worth of their inheritance, they have learned to value more highly what they have proved more fully. The same Apostolic books as gave life and strength to the early Churches, quicken our own. And they are recognised in the same way, by familiar and reverent use, and not by any formal decree."

We cannot tell what the letter *means*, without the Spirit. Nay, we cannot even tell what the letter *is*, without the Spirit.

NOTE IV. p. 20.

Probably no stronger words against indiscriminate proselytism have ever been spoken than those directed by our blessed Lord (Matt. xxiii. 15) against the authorised teachers of the religious communion to which He Himself belonged.

It will strike the careful reader of the New Testament that both our Lord and St Paul avoided as much as possible the disturbance of any *really* religious conviction entertained by their hearers.

A wonderful amount of spiritual good has been effected by men who, standing within the verge of some communion, have resisted the strenuous efforts of those in high places to thrust them out of it.

The Apostles, though the appointed teachers of a religion which was to overthrow Judaism, were Jews to the last. St Paul among Jews professed himself not only a Jew, but a Pharisee, the son of a Pharisee; though to those that were without law, he became as without law. The Pharisees probably thought him inconsistent, hypocritical, or both.

It is good to compare the lives of Pascal and Fenelon with such careers as those of Gibbon and De Dominis.

SERMON II.

Note V. p. 34.

Disguised assertions are the more dangerous, because, as they do not at first appear like assertions, there is no *primâ facie* necessity for proving them. A curious example of a disguised and unproved assertion may be found in connection with my present subject. The following passage occurs in the Preface to a well-known edition of the Greek Testament.

"Much has been recently said on the *Inspiration* of Holy Scripture.

"It may be submitted for consideration, whether it would not be wiser to abstain from disquisitions upon *modes and degrees* of Inspiration, as a subject beyond the reach of our finite faculties.

"If it be said, that this would be too diffident a course, let it be observed that it is no other than that which was pursued by our Blessed Lord Himself in His dealings with the Old Testament. He received, and delivered to the Christian Church, all the Books, and every portion of the Books, of the Old Testament, as the Word of God.

"But though He has solemnly declared that every part of the Old Testament is inspired, He never vouchsafed to say a word concerning *degrees* of Inspiration.

"Indeed, it seems a contradiction of terms, to speak of degrees in what is Divine."

Pref. to 1st Edition. p. xviii.

Dr Wordsworth then proceeds to another part of his argument. He began the above extract by recommending an abstinence from disquisitions on modes and degrees of Inspiration. At the conclusion of a few short lines, he gives us an argument by means of which he infers that to speak of degrees of Inspiration is a contradiction in terms. Is this abstaining from disquisition on the subject?

The Argument adduced is very brief, but neither lucid nor conclusive. "It seems to be a contradiction in terms, to speak of degrees in what is Divine." A more potent formula could scarcely have been devised, to exclude God from the greater part of His Universe. Are not Goodness, Order, Beauty, Divine? And do they not exist in the world around us in all imaginable degrees?

In the hope of some further explanation, we turn to Dr Wordsworth's work on Inspiration. (2nd Edit. 1851.) He there refers to a passage of St Augustine's treatise on Christian Doctrine, which he translates as follows:—

"Of the Scriptures called Canonical, those are to be *preferred* which are *received by all Churches*, and *those* are to be *placed next* which are acknowledged by the major and graver part of Christendom."

On this Dr Wordsworth remarks:—

"Now, let me enquire, can any reasonable man speak of *preference* of one Canonical Scripture, properly so called, to another? There cannot be *degrees* in *Inspiration*. There cannot be more or less in what is *Divine*. It is therefore clear that the word *Canonical* is sometimes used by Augustine in a laxer sense, so as not only to designate writings strictly speaking *inspired*, but also to embrace those which were held in reverence and read by the Church."—pp. 89, 90.

Here we see that Dr Wordsworth employs as the basis of an argument the dogma, from disquisition on which he elsewhere advises us to abstain. He assures us that St Augustine must have meant something different from the obvious meaning of his words, because there cannot be degrees in inspiration; and he tells us that there cannot be degrees in inspiration, because there cannot be more or less in what is Divine. Does Dr Wordsworth wish to say there cannot be degrees of Divine Illumination, Divine Guidance, Divine Grace?

It increases our perplexity to find the following passage in the same work of the same writer:—"Looking at the origin of the Four Gospels, and at the Divine attributes of Unity, Omniscience, Omnipotence, and Eternity, which God has in rich measure been pleased to bestow on them by His Holy Spirit, the Christian Church found a prophetic picture of them in the Four living Cherubim, named from heavenly knowledge, seen by Ezekiel at the river of Chebar."—p. 163.

It is not easy to fix any precise meaning to the opening clauses of this sentence. But surely Dr Wordsworth does not mean to imply that the Gospels possess the Divine attributes of Unity, Omniscience, Omnipotence, and Eternity, in the same measure and degree as God Himself. But if not, he must admit that there is more or less in what is Divine. Certainly, a writer who employs a deductive theory of inspiration so daringly, so unskilfully, and so unconsciously, should abstain from attributing 'assumption and conceit' to a criticism different from his own, and from accusing the patient labourer in the paths of induction of "shallow and presumptuous sciolism."—(N. T. in Acts vii.)

Note VI. p. 54.

The allusion is of course to the Second Epistle of St Peter. There seems an inclination at the present day to forget, in the heat of modern controversy, the simple facts regarding that Epistle. Those who fail to perceive the difficulties arising from its style, which Jerome saw and endeavoured to account for, may still be reminded that there are important deficiencies in the external testimony to its genuineness. It is ignored by Tertullian, Cyprian, and Clement of Alexandria. Its Petrine authorship was denied by Didymus and Eusebius, and doubted in ancient times by Origen and Amphilochius. In later times, Cajetan, Calvin, Erasmus, Grotius, Salmasius and Scaliger, revived these doubts. A recent competent judge, Mr Westcott, is of opinion that no trace can be found of its existence before A.D. 170.—(*Canon of the New Testament*, p. 367.) Probably, the Church, though unable to clear up the doubts about its authorship, had no doubt about its doctrine, and therefore admitted it into the Canon. As Eusebius remarks, "having appeared to many persons to be useful, it has received earnest attention together with the other Scriptures." While we accept it as Canonical, we may well bear in mind the spirit of the rule given by St Augustine, and quoted in the last note. A reverent sense of its difficulties will become us better than eager controversy concerning it. In this and the other Canonical books, as St Augustine reminds us in the same treatise, "those who fear God and are gentle in their piety, seek the will of God."

SERMON III.

NOTE VII. p. 58.

The latter part of this text should rather be translated, "Men spoke from God, moved by the Holy Ghost." Some early copyist probably added the epithet attributing holiness to the Prophets in general: but Balaam and Caiaphas prophesied. Nor does the text assert that the Prophets spoke as they were moved by the Holy Ghost. It rather says that the Holy Spirit moved them to speak. The two assertions, of course, are not the same. A ship moves, borne along by the wind: but it does not necessarily move as the wind moves.

NOTE VIII. p. 67.

It is scarcely necessary to remind the reader, that the Church of England has no formal decree respecting the Inspiration of Holy Scripture, and that the phrase does not occur in her formularies. The following passages approach most nearly to a precise declaration on the subject.

The Sixth Article declares that "Holy Scripture containeth all things necessary to salvation."

The Collect for the Second Sunday in Advent asserts by implication that God has "caused all Holy Scriptures to be written for our learning."

In the Service for the Ordination of Deacons, the Bishop demands of the candidates: "Do you unfeignedly believe all the Canonical Scriptures of the Old and New Testament?"

In the Service for the Ordination of Priests, the Bishop asks the candidates a longer question, which it is reasonable to suppose expands and explains the shorter form addressed to the Deacons.

"Are you persuaded that the Holy Scriptures contain sufficiently all Doctrine required of necessity for eternal salvation through faith in Jesus Christ? and are you determined, out of the said Scriptures to instruct the people committed to your charge, and to teach nothing, as required of necessity to eternal salvation, but that which you shall be persuaded may be concluded and proved by the Scripture?"

NOTE IX. p. 70.

I allude of course to the miraculous agency of the Angel at the pool of Bethesda, and to the 'woman taken in adultery.'

NOTE X. p. 70.

Acts xx. 28. 1 Tim. iii. 16; to which we may add, for another reason, Acts viii. 37. The questions about Rom. ix. 5 and Titus ii. 13 are questions of interpretation; but they may serve to illustrate the same principle.

Notes. 173

There are certain precious truths, which, if once understood and apprehended, become, to a great extent, their own evidence. The belief in our Blessed Lord's Divinity has obviously grown stronger, as the difficulty of resting the doctrine on detached texts has increased. Scripture now appeals more to the spiritual faculty in man, and less to the logical faculty, than in former times. Words that may seem a hard saying to those without, call forth the faith of His true disciples. "Now are we sure that thou knowest all things, and needest not that any man should ask thee: by this we believe that thou camest forth from God."

Note XI. p. 81.

The following portrait of the Church of England, drawn by one who looks on her from without with no undiscerning eye, has features which will repay attention.

"The spirit of this Church is not, and never has been, definite and consistent. From the beginning it repudiated the distinct guidance of any theoretical principles, however exalted, and apparently Scriptural. It held fast to its historical position, as a great Institute still living and powerful under all the corruptions which had overlaid it; and while submitting to the irresistible influence of reform which swept over it, as over other churches in the sixteenth century, it refused to be refashioned according to any new model. It broke away from the medieval bondage, under which it had always been restless, and destroyed the gross abuses which had sprung out of it; it rose in an attitude of proud and successful resistance to Rome; but in doing all this, it did not go to Scripture, as if it had once more, and entirely anew, to find there the principles either of doctrinal truth or of practical government and discipline. Scripture, indeed, was eminently the condition of its revival; but Scripture was not made anew the foundation of its existence. There was too much of old historical life in it to seek any new foundation; the new must grow out of the old, and fit itself into the old. The Church of England was to be reformed, but not reconstituted. Its life was too vast, its influence too varied, its relations too complicated,—touching the national existence in all its multiplied expressions at too many points,—to be capable of being reduced to any new and definite form in more supposed uniformity with the model of Scripture, or the simplicity of the primitive Church. Its extensive and manifold organism was to be re-animated by a new life, but not remoulded according to any arbitrary or novel theory. This spirit, at once progressive and conservative, comprehensive rather than intensive, historical, and not dogmatical, is one eminently characteristic of the English mind, and, as it appears to us, in the highest degree characteristic of the English Reformation. It is far, indeed, from being an exhaustive characteristic of it. Two distinct tendencies of a quite different character, expressly dogmatic in opposite extremes, are found running alongside this main and central tendency: on the one hand, a medieval dogmatism; on the other hand, a puritanical dogmatism. The current of religious life in England, as it moved forward and took shape in the sixteenth century, is marked by this threefold bias, which has perpetuated itself to the present time. There was then, as there remains to this day, an upper, middle, and lower tendency—a theory of High-churchism, and a theory of Low-churchism—and between these contending dogmatic movements the great confluence of what was and is the peculiar type of English Christianity—a Christianity diffusive and practical rather than direct and theoretical—elevated and sympathetic rather than zealous and energetic—Scriptural and earnest in its spirit, but undogmatic and adaptive in its form."

TULLOCH'S *Leaders of the Reformation*, pp. 241—3.

SERMON IV.
NOTE XII. p. 104.

After this sermon was preached, the Author had the pleasure of meeting with the following passage from the pen of the judicious and judicial Bishop of St David's:

"I believe that the use and the force of the argument from prophecy have undergone a great change since the time of the Apostolic preaching. With regard to Christians, it is no longer needed, nor in fact is it ever employed, in the way of *evidence*. Its use in a Christian congregation is, not to produce conviction, but to promote edification: and for this purpose it may fairly be permitted to be carried to a greater extent than in controversy with unbelievers; and, when kept within the bounds of sober judgment, and not perverted into pious trifling, may be both legitimately and profitably used, though it can teach nothing which is not to be found in the New Testament.

"But as an instrument for the conversion of the Jews, the argument from prophecy has, I believe, now lost much, not indeed of its inherent efficacy, but of the means by which it was most powerfully enforced at the period of our Lord's appearance upon earth. It had then, if I may so speak, two handles, one of which has been much loosened, while the other has entirely dropped off. The one was a general familiarity with the Messianic interpretation, which has since been lost, and which must have greatly aided the application of the argument. The other was the general expectation that the advent of the Messiah was at hand......At this day the missionary argument from prophecy in the Old Testament is no longer seconded by this most powerful auxiliary."—*Letter to Dr Rowland Williams*, pp. 75—7.

NOTE XIII. p. 106.

The *assembly* alluded to in James ii. 2 was probably held in a synagogue, of which the whole customary congregation had become Christians. Such a Christian body, having its own rulers and proper organisation (comp. James v. 14), would naturally adapt and modify the worship of the synagogue to suit its peculiar needs.

Notes. 177

NOTE XIV. p. 106.

That brief but singularly valuable document, the *Epistola ad Diognetum*, attests in the clearest manner the existence of a school in the very early Church, which renounced and repudiated the most elementary Jewish traditions. The writer of that letter appears to have been a most sincere Christian. Yet, if he had had his way, the volumes of the Old and the New Testament would scarcely have been bound together as they are at present.

NOTE XV. p. 109.

The writer would call attention to some cautious and reverent remarks on this subject by Mr Westcott (*Introduction to the Gospels*, p. 274, note). It may seem to some anxious minds a dreadful thought, that we cannot be sure of having in the Gospels the very words of Christ. Yet perhaps there is an element of unbelief, as well as of faith, in such uneasiness. The Bible can only be read to advantage in the sense of dependence on God, and, under Him, on the brethren. We must allow the messenger from God to deliver his message in his own way; and we must not be surprised if to some of our questions he is unable or unwilling to answer. That form of words, which sufficed St John in expressing the truth, must suffice us in receiving it. We cannot push his personality aside, press by him, and stand nearer to Christ than he did. If he blends, with the words of his

Master, the impression which those words made on him, we, in proportion as we enter into his spirit, shall hear Christ as he heard Him. Thus much seems certain, that any view of Holy Scripture which makes it a document capable of intellectual interpretation, and not the voice of God speaking to man and through man, destroys the "Good Tidings" of the Gospel, and brings us back to a Law.

NOTE XVI. p. 110.

"*Condescended, in some real sense, to the veil of our ignorance.*" These words in the text are meant to express, in a generalised form, the truth which seems implied in the passages of Holy Scripture quoted in the context, and not to add anything to that truth.

Christ, we learn, in the truth of our nature was made like unto us in all things, sin only except. It appears that He accepted, as man, the necessary limitations of human knowledge. What these limitations are, it must be exceedingly difficult for man himself to decide; nor does the point seem to be one of those on which Holy Scripture is meant to instruct us.

A wise man instinctively accommodates his mind to that of a child when he is teaching. Yet he would find it hard to explain to a child, or even to himself, the nature of this accommodation. But the difference between the wisest man and the simplest child is as nothing to the difference between God and man; and our Lord not only taught as man, but became man. The nature of His human knowledge is therefore most inadequately represented by the analogy of a wise man teaching a child. To make the cases a little more parallel, we must suppose the wise man actually to *become* a child. If we enquire further into this mysterious subject, it should be remembered that we are in the place, not of the wise man, but of children.

NOTE XVII. p. 113.

It is happily no part of the writer's duty, and it is certainly not his inclination, to sit in judgment either on the opinions or temper of others. But he cannot help regretting that good men should so often apparently forget, that others can differ from them on hard historical questions, and yet be lovers of peace, and truth, and Christ.

If the writer were called upon to name any one person who has received but an ill return for earnest, faithful, and conscientious labour bestowed on the Old Testament, he would mention, with much respect, the name of Dr Davidson. *Talis cum sis, utinam noster esses.*

NOTE XVIII. p. 119.

See Note VIII. It has been often remarked that the word Inspiration is employed in the Prayer-book only to express the action of the Holy Spirit on the mind and heart of the believer. It has not been so often observed that even in these instances the word is of comparatively recent introduction. It occurs in the Ante-Communion Collect, and in the Collect for the fifth Sunday after Easter. In the first of these places, the Latin of the Sarum Liturgy has *infusio;* in the second, the Latin is *Te inspirante.* The term occurs twice in our English Bibles. In one of these passages (Job xxxii. 8) its use is exactly the same as in the Prayer-book: "There is a spirit in man; and the inspiration of the Almighty giveth them understanding." The other place is the important text, 2 Tim. iii. 16, in which, as appears from Note I., the word is introduced only by a partial mistranslation. There seems to be no Greek word answering to Inspiration in a theological sense: Θεοπνευστία is, I believe, a mere barbarism.

Abstract terms have undoubtedly their use, but they are often very misleading. Persons are continually disputing what is meant by Inspiration, without having previously agreed whether they are considering the inspiration of a man or of a book.

When we assert the Inspiration of Holy Scripture, we assert that through the Scripture the Holy Spirit holds converse with our spirit. A *theory* of Inspiration is an endeavour to account for this admitted fact. Most of these theories insist very strongly on the Inspiration of the human authors, that is, on the mental and spiritual condition of certain speakers or writers, to whom we owe the text of Holy Scripture. About *this* Inspiration also there are many theories. Happily, the fact of the Inspiration of Holy Scripture is independent of them all.

Every abstract term introduced into theology, if it has a tendency to obscure the personal nature of religion, is so far an evil. Probably, no abstract term is more free from this danger than *Trinity*. It expresses, we know, a threefoldness of *Persons;* and we are carefully taught to regard the Father, the Son, and Holy Spirit as standing in a personal relation to ourselves, as Creator, Redeemer, and Sanctifier. Yet it would be a terrible symptom of spiritual deadness, if *Trinity*, or even *Deity*, were a common substitute in our worship for the simple name of God.

THE END.

www.ingramcontent.com/pod-product-compliance
Lightning Source LLC
Chambersburg PA
CBHW051056160426
43193CB00010B/1203